For Birth, Postpartum & End-of-Life Doulas

The
Doula Business Guide
Workbook
Tools to Create a Thriving Practice
3rd Edition

By Patty Brennan

The Doula Business Guide, 3rd Edition and *The Doula Business Guide Workbook, 3rd Edition* are available for purchase from Lifespan Doulas [LifespanDoulas.com]. A 40% wholesale discount is available for orders of six or more copies of a book.

ISBN 978-0-9797247-4-9

With Gratitude To

Catherine Fischer,
Harriette Hartigan,
Monique Kulick and
Barbara Robertson

— past and present members of my Mastermind group
for their amazing capacity to listen, gently critique,
share insights and make suggestions

Table of Contents

Preface

The notion that heart-centered work and making money are somehow fundamentally incompatible is a false dichotomy. You *can* choose a path of service to others *and* thrive financially. In fact, it is essential that you do so or, more likely than not, you will be forced to give up the work altogether—a lose/lose proposition.

This *Workbook* is designed to complement my book *The Doula Business Guide: How to Succeed as a Birth, Postpartum or End-of-Life Doula, 3rd Edition,* which is a comprehensive overview of the business side of being a doula. You will find a variety of interactive success tools, appropriate for both new and veteran doula business owners. Emphasis is placed on making measurable progress towards your goals with our checklists, step-by-step instructions, tips sheets, worksheets, implementation exercises, questionnaires, strategies, planners and more. The *Workbook* is organized into four sections—Dream, Organize, Plan and Grow. Feel free to jump in anywhere you like, adopting a non-linear and playful approach. When there is so much that needs to be done, it's okay to give yourself permission to do what feels most engaging first. Launching your business will be an ongoing creative process, though some of the more mundane aspects of putting infrastructure in place (e.g., developing client forms, setting up your bookkeeping) only need to be done once and, if done right, will serve you well for years to come.

To become a successful business owner, it's critical to understand who your customers are and to identify factors that drive their purchasing decisions. You are encouraged to take the time to be thoughtful and explicit here. The reward for your efforts will be a heightened ability to connect with your ideal customers, craft meaningful messages to them and make competition moot. This central theme is incorporated through a few of the tools.

The main idea is this: All entrepreneurs must invest some time working *on* their business, not just *in* their business. Don't get me wrong … your doula skills and nurturing personality are supremely important. Being the best doula you can be is job number one. But if you do not also embrace marketing and learn the related skills in that field, then you aren't likely to attract the number of clients you require, over time, to meet your income needs. We must endeavor to see ourselves as business owners, professional and success-oriented, in addition to being doulas. The reality that this is a process cannot be over-emphasized. It takes time to progress from novice to expert, as Amy Gilliland details in her *Doulaing the Doula* blog [AmyGilliland.com]. Stage one is the novice doula; stage two, the advanced beginner doula; stage three, the seasoned or competent doula; stage four, the proficient doula; and finally, stage five, the expert doula. Phew! And that's just the doula service aspect of your chosen career.

The creation of a business from the ground up is an ongoing multi-faceted challenge. For me, it has been the work of a lifetime. I trust that this *Workbook* will help you to embrace it.

Part 1

Dream

Personal Inventory

Introduction

All small business owners need to wear different hats. It's not enough to just be good at what you do to be successful (though that is a huge part of it!). A variety of other skills and personal assets are needed. If you can maximize your strengths and undertake whatever is necessary to address your weaknesses, then you will increase your chances of success over time. Becoming self-aware is the first step, so I invite you to view yourself through this critical lens.

If you find that you have identified significant deficits at the end of this process, remember that you are just seeing a snapshot of where you are at this moment in time. It is not a definition of your capacities. You and your business will always be a work in progress. Sometimes, we just need the proper motivation to undertake learning a new skill or gaining mastery over personal habits that do not serve us well. Finding our niche in life, our passion, together with the need to make a living can provide the motivation that previously eluded us. It is okay to play to your strengths as well, so don't feel too daunted. With an abundance of items on my "to do" list, I can often overcome inertia by going for the low-hanging fruit—those things that feel easy for me. However, experience has taught me a few lessons: (1) procrastination is way more trouble than tackling the task at hand; (2) I don't have to personally accomplish everything that may be required—I can hire (or barter for) help; and (3) I can learn new skills or develop new habits. If we can become conscious and self-aware, then we can proceed in a much more effective, efficient and frugal manner.

Checklist

Rate yourself on a scale of 1 to 5 for each item, as follows:

> *1 = very weak, basically non-existent*
> *2 = somewhat weak, needs work*
> *3 = acceptable*
> *4 = good*
> *5 = strong, excellent*

Business-Related Skills

- Writing (grammar, spelling, clarity) ____
- Verbal communication ____
- Public speaking ____
- Artistic ____
- Organizational ____
- Money management ____
- Good at setting and maintaining professional boundaries ____

Personal strengths

- Able to establish rapport, connect with others ____
- Integrity (follow through on promises, reliable, trustworthy) ____
- Sense of humor ____

- Resourceful   ____
- Persistent   ____
- Enthusiastic, passionate   ____
- Positive, optimistic outlook on life, sees possibilities   ____
- Efficient use of time   ____
- Frugal (careful use of money)   ____
- Hard working, strong work ethic   ____
- High self-esteem   ____
- Courageous (willing to get out of my comfort zone)   ____
- Balanced   ____

Habits
- Timely   ____
- Self-disciplined   ____
- Able to set goals and meet them   ____
- Focused   ____
- Love to read and learn   ____

Assets
- Money (ability to pay for training, supplies, start-up)   ____
- Computer/printer access   ____
- Vehicle in good working order   ____
- Community connections, friendships, networks   ____
- Family support   ____

Motivation
- Love for what you do   ____
- Creativity   ____
- Money   ____
- Service to others   ____
- Political/idealistic (make the world a better place)   ____
- Enjoy working   ____

Reflections

Skills and knowledge
Think about how your strengths (4s and 5s) might be used in developing your business. How can you accentuate these? Where/how will they be put to best use?

Are there any 1s or 2s? How important are these skills for developing your business? Where and when might they hold you back?

What steps can you take to prevent a lack in one area from leading to an overall negative impression from the perspective of your future clients?

Is there a skill you want to gain? Identify the steps needed to do so.

Do you need to identify a source of help?

Personal Strengths
Celebrate your strengths (4s and 5s)! How will these serve you well in growing your business?

Which of the qualities on this list do you imagine are most essential for being successful in your business?

Which of the qualities on this list would you most like to acquire or strengthen? What steps can you take to make that a reality? (TIP: Bring your attention to that quality each day, in a positive way—study it, inspirational reading, discuss with a friend, visualization, affirmations, spiritual practices).

Habits
We all struggle with habits, both good and bad. Which ones will serve you well as you build your business?

Where might you get into trouble?

What can you do about any limitations? (Change the script, perhaps? For example, set one small goal and achieve it; and then another; now you have become someone who sets goals and achieves them. Your past is not your future!)

Assets
What are your business assets?

Do you have what you bottom-line need to do your work (e.g., reliable transportation, child care, time)?

If your answer is no to the above question, can you think outside the box about how to get your needs met?

Motivations
Our motivations keep us going. Frankly, the incentive to make money can be a powerful motivator. Without it, you may find that your "business" is more of a hobby. How can you keep your motivation high?

Wrap-Up

Take a step back and look at the big picture. What skills, personal strengths, habits, assets and motivations should you seek to maximize as you develop your business?

What are your top three biggest liabilities?

What capacities might you need to acquire? What new skills might you need to learn to overcome these limitations?

As you reflect on your weak areas, is there anything here you can outsource, that someone else can do for you?

Examining Our Beliefs about Money Exercise

8 Limiting Beliefs about Money

1. Money is the root of all evil.

2. The amount of money available is limited.

3. It is more spiritual to be poor.

4. One must work hard for money.

5. If my work is fun and I love it, then it is not worth much.

6. I'm just not good with money.

7. I never have enough money.

8. Someone else will provide for me.

Personal Exercise

Do you agree with or sometimes think any of the above? What are your deep beliefs about money?

What is the basis of your beliefs? Where did they come from? Who are your influences?

Is your relationship to money a positive force in your life? If not, can you begin to cultivate new thoughts, influences, beliefs, choices, behaviors—in a sense, re-program yourself?

On the next page, you will see statements that represent a scarcity mindset. Do you identify with any of these? If so, write an abundance affirmation to counteract your limiting beliefs and behaviors. The more you can focus on the right-hand column rather than indulging your scarcity mindset the better!

Scarcity versus Abundance Worksheet

Scarcity Mindset	Abundance Affirmations
You feel utterly crushed because a prospective client chose to hire another doula.	
A new, business-savvy doula moves to town and sets up her/his practice. You feel annoyed.	
You discover that a relatively inexperienced doula is charging significantly more than you are. You complain to a business associate.	
You worry that your community is overly saturated with doulas.	
You feel jealous of another doula who is prospering in her/his business. She/he seems to have endless resources to make a beautiful website, create a beautiful office space, etc.	
You are filled with worry and stress about money issues. Adrenaline is flooding your system.	
You are lacking in confidence about your doula practice, not sure if you are good enough, experienced enough, etc.	

"When resources are perceived to be limited, paranoia,
fear and politics thrive."

~ John C. Maxwell

Where do you dwell?

SCARCITY

ABUNDANCE

worry, stress, negativity, jealousy, anger, irritability, complaining, isolation, revengeful, aggressive, failing, manipulative, loser, adversarial, stingy, power-grabbing, desperation

confidence, allies, peace, satisfaction, persistence resilience, generosity, self-acceptance, caring interactions, generosity of spirit, positive reputation, learns from mistakes, collaboration, inspired and inspiring

Ideas for changing a deeply-held limiting belief or ingrained pattern:

One can't simply snap one's fingers and say, "be gone." It's a process and processes inherently mandate time. (We know this as doulas, right? One can't suddenly "be healed" and return to normal after birth; healing takes time. Birthing and dying aren't results; they are processes and patience is often required.)

Doula, doula thyself!
You can do this. You *are* doing this.

1. **Dis-invest.** The process of dis-investing begins by bringing our attention to the belief, behavior or pattern; e.g., noticing when the belief that we don't have enough (or we're not physically attractive, or don't make friends easily, etc.) is operative in our thinking, mood, choices.

2. **Objectification.** Next, begin by stepping outside of yourself to perceive the limiting belief as an entity that is separate from you. Name it, don't own it ("There's my fear again" rather than "I feel afraid"). This begins the process of robbing power from the belief. Stick with it. If you find yourself relapsing, not to worry. In some perverse way, this is your comfort zone. At one earlier point in time, you probably had good reasons for responding this way. No need to be harsh with yourself, just keep paying attention. Be curious. What are the triggers? What are the associated emotions? You are beginning to disengage. Perhaps journaling about your process of self-discovery will help?

3. **Transcend.** Next, consider what supports might help you to transcend this belief or pattern in your life. Immersing yourself in the self-help book genre? Mindfulness training? Listening to inspirational programs while driving? Posting affirmations where you can see them regularly? Or perhaps counseling is needed because there really is a truckload of childhood baggage and deep feelings of unworthiness weighing you down and it's time to put them in the past? (Remember, the healthiest member of the family is often the one who seeks help.)

Affirmations Answer Key

Just in case you struggled to come up with affirmations in the preceding worksheet, I am providing sample affirmations below.

Scarcity Mindset	Abundance Affirmations
You feel utterly crushed because a prospective client chose to hire another doula.	"I am attracting the clients that are right for me."
A new, business-savvy doula moves to town and sets up her/his practice. You feel annoyed.	"There's always room at the top." "Competition is moot." "There is plenty of work for all."
You discover that a relatively inexperienced doula is charging significantly more than you are. You complain to a business associate.	"I am comfortable with my fees." "I know my own value." "I am focused on my success."
You worry that your community is overly saturated with doulas.	"Word of mouth about the benefits of doulas is growing!" "I have a fabulous community of doulas and all the help I need."
You feel jealous of another doula who appears to be prospering in her/his business. She/he seems to have endless resources to make a beautiful website, create a beautiful office space, etc.	"I am enough." "I am in the perfect place for me at this moment." "I am inspired to be my best."
You are filled with worry and stress about money issues. Adrenaline is flooding your system.	"I always have what I need." "Money is flowing to me." "My efforts are paying off."
You are lacking in confidence about your doula practice, not sure if you are good enough, experienced enough, etc.	"I am enough." "I am doing my very best for each client." "I have unique gifts."

Suggestions for Working with Affirmations

Much of our life has a self-fulfilling character. We seem to attract what we fear, or we can often say, "I knew that would happen to me." Since what we say about ourselves (positive or negative) strongly influences what unfolds in our lives, it is possible to use this natural law consciously to our advantage via positive affirmations. Repeating or writing affirmations can help you to realize their truth and to identify and release any blocks from the past that may stand in the way of these statements manifesting in your life. By employing affirmations, we can reprogram deep-seated, often subconscious patterns in our lives that are not serving us well.

- Work with one or more every day. The best times are just before sleeping, before starting the day or when you are feeling troubled.

- Write each affirmation 10 or 20 times on a sheet of paper, leaving space in the right-hand margin of the page for the "emotional response." As you write the affirmation down on the left side of the page, jot down whatever thoughts, considerations, beliefs, fears or emotions come to your mind. Keep repeating the affirmation and notice how the responses on the right change.

- Put specific names and situations into the affirmation. Include your name in the affirmation. Say and write each affirmation in the first, second and third person. "I (your name) love myself. You (your name) love yourself. (Your name) now loves herself."

- Play with the vocabulary in the affirmation. Make it personal and meaningful. Be specific about your desired result.

- Record your affirmations and play them back when you can. A good time is while driving or when going to bed.

- Try looking in the mirror and saying the affirmations to yourself out loud. Keep saying them until you see yourself with a relaxed, happy expression. Keep saying them until you eliminate all facial tension and grimaces.

- Sit across from a partner, each of you in a straight chair with your hands on your thighs and knees barely touching. Say the affirmation to your partner until you are comfortable doing it. Your partner can observe your body language carefully. If you squirm, fidget or are unclear, you do not pass. He or she should not allow you to go on until you say the affirmation very clearly, without contrary body reactions and upsets. Then your partner says them back to you, using the second person and your name. Continue until you can receive them without embarrassment. This is harder than it sounds!

- Don't give up! If you ever get to a point where you begin to feel upset, shaky or afraid about something negative you discover, don't panic. Keep on writing the applicable affirmation over and over until your mind takes on a new thought. As it does, the negativity will fade away and you will feel lighter and better. Remember, it is just as easy to think positively as negatively. In fact, it is easier. Negative thinking takes more effort.

- Don't be afraid to experiment. Affirmations can be useful in all areas of your life—for problems at work, problems with health, personal growth ...

Crafting a Mission Statement

A Mission Statement is a short, powerful statement articulating the overarching purpose of your business. Crafting a Mission Statement is a process and it has value for its own sake, beyond the result. The process invites you to articulate why you do this work. What inspires you and fuels your passion? Over time, your Mission Statement will help you stay focused and provide guidance for future growth. Most successful small business owners are creative people. We do not suffer from a lack of good ideas. But it is hard at times to know which ideas are worth pursuing, which might best be placed on the back burner at any given time. When considering the addition of new programs, services or avenues for expansion, the business owner can ask herself, "Does it serve the mission?" "Has my mission changed?" If the answer to the latter question is yes, then it is time to revisit the Mission Statement and acknowledge that your purpose or focus has evolved into something new.

For Consideration

1. Why are you in business? What do you want for yourself, your family and your customers? Think about the spark that ignited your decision to start a doula business.

2. Who are you serving? What are the benefits of hiring a doula? What can you do for your customers that will enrich their lives—now and in the future?

3. What image of your business do you want to convey? Customers, employees (if any) and the public will all have perceptions of your company. How will you create the desired picture?

4. What products or services do you offer? What factors determine pricing and quality?

5. How do you differ from your competitors? Define what makes you and your service extraordinary.

Tips for Writing the Mission Statement

- Take your answers to the above questions and distill them down to their essence, eliminating any wordiness. Be ruthless here, especially when it comes to jettisoning hype that everybody claims. Cut as much as you can that isn't unique to your business.

- Now, make it flow. Give the statement a bit of polish using colorful, dynamic language. What emotion does it evoke? Is it compelling? Every word matters.

- Involve anyone who may be connected to your business to weigh in. Even (especially?) if you are a sole proprietor, it's always helpful to get feedback from others. Invariably, others will see what you miss, help you question your assumptions and generally make it better.

- Keep in mind that it is more challenging to write a short versus a longer statement. If you write some great stuff that gets cut, perhaps it can be repurposed elsewhere (e.g., on your website, in a blog or in promotional materials).

Sample Mission Statements

The following samples should give you an idea. These samples are not all equally compelling. You be the judge.

A childbirth education business:
> To inform and inspire expectant parents to realize their own best vision for a healthy and joyful passage into parenthood.

A perinatal hospice nonprofit:
> To provide support, education and encouragement to families who choose to carry their dying baby to term.

A community-based nonprofit for teens:
> To help young people lead safe, healthy and productive lives through intensive intervention and prevention services.

A doula collective:
> To enhance the physical, emotional, psychological and spiritual health of mothers, babies and families through education and loving support during pregnancy, childbirth and early parenthood.

A women's center:
> To promote self-determination for women and families by providing professional services that build confidence, strengthen connections and create positive change.

Articulating Your Vision

A Vision Statement affirms your destination. When you put it all together, what change has been created? Your vision may be idealistic, inspirational or personal. It might focus on the greater good or making more money for your family. You may choose to share it with others or hold it for yourself as a kind of compass. State your vision in positive terms as a done deal. One thing I have observed is that the more specific we are about our intentions, the more likely we are to manifest them in our life. What are you intending to accomplish through your work?

Sample Vision Statements

Organizational:
- Every family who wants a doula has access to one.
- Provide comprehensive birth and postpartum doula services and childbirth preparation classes.
- Host a thriving community space where new parents and their babies can gather for support, education and fun.
- Provide comprehensive support services at the end of life so that people who want to die at home can do so.

Personal:

- In three years, I will be making an annual net income of $_____ from my doula business.
- Joyful engagement with financially rewarding work.

Identifying Your Core Values

Core values are the ideas, beliefs and principles underlying the mission. A statement of core values articulates your philosophy of service, why you do what you do. For example, the perinatal hospice in our sample mission statements exists "to provide support, education and encouragement to families who choose to carry their dying baby to term." Why?

Our core values will be reflected in every aspect of how we provide services—the classes we teach; products we offer; how we treat customers, employees and competitors; and so on. Articulating your core values makes your biases transparent. This in turn provides a great filter for the consumer. If they hold similar values, then they will be attracted to you. If their values are in opposition to yours, then (thankfully) they will seek services elsewhere. You can't be all things to all people. Don't be afraid to stand for what you believe. In marketing language, this is your brand.

Sample Statements of Core Values

The perinatal hospice nonprofit:
> We believe that every dying person deserves dignity and respect, and that one's value does not depend on length of life.

Center for the Childbearing Year [center4cby.com]:
- *Birth matters.* We believe that the quality and experience of birth and early parenthood have far-reaching consequences for individuals, families and society.
- *Pregnancy and birth are normal life events.* We promote the midwifery model of care as optimal for mothers and babies.
- *Breastfeeding is best for moms and babies.* We encourage all mothers to breastfeed and endorse the Ten Steps to Successful Breastfeeding of the Baby-Friendly Hospital Initiative as developed by WHO-UNICEF.
- *Education is empowerment.* We provide evidence-based information that encourages informed decision-making, preventive action, holistic approaches and an attitude of personal responsibility towards family health.

What are your Core Values? Consider …

Questions for All Doulas

Do you see yourself as holistic-minded, looking favorably on alternative health care modalities? Or do you resonate more with the mainstream medical model?

Do you limit or target services to a specific population or demographic? Why?

How do your spiritual beliefs inform your doula work? Do you intend that your spiritual beliefs will be transparent to your clients?

List three words that best represent your most important values in your doula work.

Questions for Birth and Postpartum Doulas

Why does the birth experience matter?

Do you favor a specific approach to birth? Why?

What are your views on breastfeeding?

What are your beliefs and values regarding parenting? (Right way? Wrong way?)

Are there specific birth and parenting methods, trends, movements that you endorse?

Questions for End-of-Life Doulas

What is your idea of a "good death"?

Do you favor a specific approach to death and the doula's role? Describe briefly the key components of your approach.

What are your views on natural after death care (e.g., home funerals, green burial)?

Are there specific spiritual practices or rituals that you incorporate in your doula services?

Are there specific trends in end-of-life care that you endorse?

It is not necessary, or recommended, to explicitly answer each of these questions in a statement of core values. Rather, the questions are intended to prompt reflection on your beliefs and preferences. What are you passionate about? What is important to you? Why do you do what you do? *Decide what you stand for.*

Your statement of core values can be as simple as one sentence or it may contain several points. If another organization has perfectly articulated a set of values, standards or recommendations that you favor, then you can state your endorsement and link to their statement(s). For doulas, it may be as simple as citing the standards of practice and code of ethics for doulas published by the professional training and certification agency with whom you are affiliated. Or you can use the doula scope of practice as a jumping off point and make it more authentically your own.

Once you are fully conscious of the values that underlie your approach to doula work, you can decide how or where you might make your values transparent to your customers. Here are some options:

- Publish your statement of core values on your website.
- Include your statement in an information packet for folks who have inquired about your services.
- Distill your core values into a few simple words that can be used as a tagline for your business.
- Blog about the various core values that you hold.
- Set your statement aside for now and consult later as you begin to develop your "messaging."

Whatever you decide, and whether you even take the time to articulate them or not, your core values will inform and be reflected in all aspects of your business and the support services you provide. This process encourages you to use your values intentionally to build your brand.

Lifespan Doulas
[LifespanDoulas.com]

Our Mission

Our mission is to provide professional training and development
for end-of-life doulas.

Our Vision

Our vision is for end-of-life doulas to become mainstreamed in our culture
so that everyone will have knowledge about and access to
the services of a trained end-of-life doula.

Our Core Values and Beliefs

Death is understood to be a normal life event, not just an abrupt ending.

The Doula Model of Care offers a holistic model of support
perfectly suited to the end of life.

Holistic care is defined as addressing the needs of the whole person,
including physical, emotional, psychological, social,
cultural and spiritual aspects.

Doulas serve both the dying person and their family members and loved ones.

The dying person and family will benefit from information and resources
that encourage consideration of available choices and pro-active
planning based on their values and preferences.

Doulas provide non-judgmental, confidential and respectful support
adapted to the unique needs of each family served.

Part 2

Organize

Getting Organized

Step One. Declutter

One of my college roommates was a constant reminder of the self-created hell of being organizationally impaired. To be fair, I knew (let's call her) Mary's tendencies before agreeing to be her roommate so I'm not complaining or making a moral judgment here. Mary owned a bunch of cute clothes, but they were never in any shape to be worn because they lived in heaps on the floor. Getting ready for a Saturday night date was a sad series of frustrations as one lovely outfit after another was dug from the heaps and found wanting. At one point, she took up decoupage and, subsequently, an open can of varnish and half-finished craft projects were added to the mix. Of course, the varnish spilled and ruined the clothes. I remember thinking that it just wasn't that hard to *not* throw everything into a heap. The various dramas resulting from never being able to find anything she needed, or having it ruined when she did find it, resulted in her being chronically late. It had a snowball effect.

As a small business owner, I guarantee that being utterly disorganized in your habits will get in the way of your success. What good is a doula who can't find her keys when it's time to go to a birth or a death vigil? And that's just the tip of the iceberg. You at least need a corner of a room that you can claim for your business. Perhaps a desk, computer, printer, bookcase and file cabinet. Let's get started with decluttering.

Get three large boxes and sort what's in the room. Everything can be assigned to one of three categories:

If this is too daunting, set a timer and just sort in short bursts, but keep at it. (One expert suggests sorting just ten items at a time.) The Throw Out box is the easiest. Just do it. Your Give Away box may need a bit more sorting (return to owner, donate, etc.), but you will get there, piece-by-piece. Finally, your Keep Box is where the real work begins. It's likely your Keep Box will contain items requiring action—some relatively easy to dispatch (e.g., pay a bill) and others that feel more annoying or time-consuming leading to entrenched procrastination (e.g., calling AT&T to get a better rate or creating a filing system for important papers from scratch). This leads to Step Two.

> Guiding Decision Principle:
>
> Have I used this item in the last three years?
> If not, then perhaps it's time to let it go.

Step Two. Implement a system for handling information.

Tangible stuff. Do you have a heap of papers that you plan to get to "someday" while meanwhile they form a black hole that continuously sucks more and more into the abyss? Are these items distributed through every room in your house? If so, return to Step One. Once you have your Keep Box full, it's time to find a place for everything. And that's just the tangible, "stuff" part of the equation. Here is where your book shelf and file cabinet come into play. These don't need to be new acquisitions by the way. I have picked up two-drawer file cabinets for $10 at yard sales.

Intangible stuff. What about all that virtual information that you are creating or that comes through daily? How efficient are you at keeping it organized and accessible for when you need it? Take the following quiz.

Is my computer a disaster zone?	Yes / No
Do you store random Word files all over your desktop?	____ / ____
Does your Inbox routinely have hundreds of emails in it?	____ / ____
Do you regularly spend time looking for lost documents, etc.?	____ / ____
Have you "lost" something important in the last month?	____ / ____

If you have two or more "yes" responses here, you need an intervention. It appears that you may not really understand your tools, and this is undoubtedly leading to wasted time and effort. An investment of time *now* to get things properly set up will pay huge dividends later. As your business grows (that's what we're aiming for, right?), your computer skills and infrastructure will support that growth. It's fine if you only have twenty Word documents and want to store them on your desktop, but it's not fine when you have hundreds or thousands of documents. Perhaps your cluttered Inbox "system" works for you now, but email programs are not designed to hold thousands of emails in the Inbox. Eventually, such an overload will crash the program. Plus, how can you tell what is important or still pending with your non-system?

Since there are so many different devices and programs, I cannot give you step-by-step advice regarding how to solve the problem(s). Some general solutions for procuring help follow:

- Ask a more computer-savvy friend or family member to sit with you and show you how to use some of the various organizational systems on your computer, such as Windows Explorer for sorting Word and picture files. Have them show you how to create new file folders and move the documents into your virtual file cabinet. Other tools include using the "bookmarks" function in your browser or "canned responses" in Gmail. Ultimately, these tools are significant time-savers.

- Hire a private computer consultant to help you. My husband does this for a living (this is how I know about the downstream effects of the over-stuffed Inbox). He charges $80 per hour to go to private homes and small businesses to fix folks' computers. Often, the "fix" involves showing people how to use their computers properly. Bad browsing habits on the net or lack of a backup system can get you in real trouble. Have someone look at the big picture of how you are set up.

- Identify the issue that is causing the greatest loss of your time and tackle that one first. Once you understand your new system and have integrated it into daily use, then you are ready to resolve the next problem on your list.

Purge once a year

I have been told by more than one person in my life that I am the most organized person they have ever met, so this is one of my strengths (not withstanding an OCD component that might occasionally put it over the top). Nevertheless, when in a hurry, I might randomly put Word files in the wrong folder or duplicate efforts. So, I find that at least once a year, it's beneficial to open every file folder and clean things up a bit. This is where an Archives folder comes into play. I don't want to toss that 2018 class registration database (you never know when you might need to look something up), but I also don't really need my current class database to have hundreds of old entries in it that make it more unwieldly. So, I start a new one for 2019 and archive the old one. In my purging process, some documents might get renamed or deleted, folders might get merged or new ones created, and so on. Any system is useful only to the degree that you use it and maintain it and know where to look for needed items.

You will also benefit from purging the tangible stuff—going through your paper files and tossing stuff you no longer need or archiving what you do (e.g., tax-related receipts). Clearly, this all takes time, but is much less daunting when maintained on a regular basis. Otherwise, entropy inevitably sets in. Have you ever seen those pictures where the jungle swallowed up an entire temple, hidden to human eye? That's entropy. Nobody fought the jungle back.

> In his best-selling book, *12 Rules for Life*, Jordan Peterson urges us to ask ourselves,
>
> "What *could* I do, that I *would* do, to make Life a little better?"

Business Name Quiz
Is it good? Is it available? Does it help with my SEO?

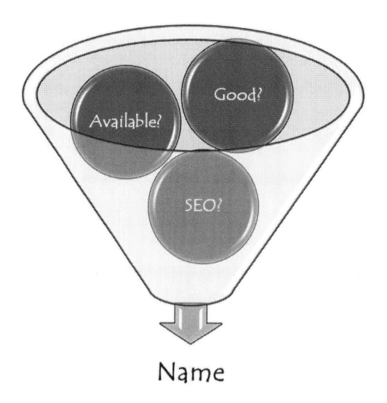

Name

Is it a good name?

	Agree	Disagree
1. I sometimes need to explain my business name to others.	____	____
2. My business name is difficult for others to spell.	____	____
3. My business name leaves folks guessing what I do.	____	____
4. My name is very similar to another business.	____	____
5. My name limits future growth (e.g., addition of new services).	____	____

If you "agree" with any of the above questions, you may want to re-think your name.

To Do: Ask at least 10 other people (some who know what you do and some who may not) what they think of your proposed business name. Or, give them a choice of two or three names and ask them to vote.

Is your proposed name available?

1. If you plan to incorporate, then you will need to conduct a business name search on your state's website. If the name has been taken or is like a protected name, then it will not be accepted.
2. If you plan to operate as a sole proprietor under a DBA ("Doing Business As"; also referred to as an "assumed name"), then do a business name search on your county's government website to determine local availability.
3. What will be the corresponding URL for your website? Is that URL available as a dot.com?
4. Is your business name available on Facebook?

You'll want to reserve the dot.com version of your name as this is what most people will enter first in the search engines. If you use the dot.net variation, for example, then you may be unintentionally driving traffic to a competitor. The dot.org variation designates a nonprofit organization. It's actually a good idea to buy all three primary domain name variations to ensure the most thorough protection.

To Do:
1. Once you have settled on a name and determined that it is available, go ahead and protect it by incorporating (state level protection), securing the DBA (county level protection) or federal trademark (national level protection; expensive and probably not necessary for local business owners).
2. Once you have settled on a URL, go ahead and reserve your domain name, even if you are not ready to develop your website. Once you do have a website, the variations can redirect folks to your dot.com homepage.
3. Protect your name and brand on Facebook by creating a business page. Again, you do not have to develop the page at this time; just reserve it so no one else can snatch it up. If you do not already have a personal profile on Facebook, then you will need to create one before you can create a business page. Facebook will not allow your page to be inactive indefinitely however, but they will give you a warning if you go too long without engagement on the forum.

Does your name help you with your Search Engine Optimization (SEO)?

1. Are your primary keywords incorporated in your business name?
2. Are your primary keywords incorporated in your URL?

If your answer to either of these questions is "no," it is not necessarily a deal breaker, but it is worth reconsidering. A name like "Ann Arbor Doulas" (domain name AnnArborDoulas.com) may not be the most evocative emotionally, or the most interesting from a creative standpoint, but it sure makes up for those shortcomings with its powerful SEO potential, driving visitors to the site.

Summary

Naming your business is not a straightforward, linear process. It can be really discouraging to focus all your efforts on generating an awesome business name only to find that someone else beat you to it. And, as more and more domain names get snatched up, it becomes increasingly challenging to be unique. You will need to be simultaneously moving back and forth between these three sets of considerations until it all comes together. Have fun with it and good luck!

For further guidance and tips on choosing a business name and branding your business, see *The Doula Business Guide, 3rd Edition.*

Comparison of Doula Business Models
Which model best suits your skills and personality?

Comparison Parameters		Independent Doula	Doula Partnership	Doula Collective	Doula Agency Owner	Agency Doula
Peer Support	Camaraderie, not being isolated	Doing your own thing; may feel isolated	Sharing everything with your partner(s)	Doing your own thing AND collaborating	Lots of interaction	Part of a group
	Ease of backup	Must arrange on your own	Shared on-call	Backup by group members	Set policy	Backup provided
	Time off call	Up to you; arrange backup or refrain from taking clients	Yes	Variable; depends on the group	Always responsible for business	Depends on policies; doulas accept assignments on a case-by-case basis
Degree of Control	Control over business decisions	Complete control	Shared equally with partner(s)	Complete control over your own business; consensus on group operations	Complete control	No control
	Speed of decision making	As slow or fast as you alone are capable	Slower due to need to come to agreement; more partners yield a slower process	Slow; more members yield a slower process; challenge of getting group members together	As slow or fast as you alone are capable	N/A

Comparison Parameters		Independent Doula	Doula Partnership	Doula Collective	Doula Agency Owner	Agency Doula
Degree of Control (continued)	Control over choice of clients, backup	Complete control	Shared with partner	Good control; depends somewhat on group policies	Complete control	Variable; depends on policies but often matches are made and doulas assigned
	Accountability (who responsible to?)	Responsible to self and clients only	Responsible to self, partner(s) and clients	Responsible to self, group members and clients	Responsible to self, agency doulas and clients	Responsible to self, agency owner, potentially other doulas (e.g., if working in teams) and clients
	Job security	High, if … *	High, if …	High, if …	High, if …	Medium (can be fired or agency can stop making referrals any time)
Simple vs. Complex	Getting set up	Complex; solely responsible for everything	Potentially easier since you can split the tasks; however more complex as you negotiate all aspects of the partnership agreement	May be relatively simple if you are joining a well-established existing collective	Complex; lots of decisions and tasks	Simple; few responsibilities; if independent contractor, then responsible for that piece

Comparison Parameters		Independent Doula	Doula Partnership	Doula Collective	Doula Agency Owner	Agency Doula
Simple vs. Complex (continued)	Ongoing administrative tasks	Everything is up to you	Split equally with partners (theoretically)	Depends on what the group decides	Everything is up to you	Relatively little; just what the owner requires
	Communication challenges	Very little; responsible to communicate with clients, backup doulas	Challenges increase with number of partners	High potential for issues; increases with number of group members	Complex; lots of people to communicate with and manage	Medium; communicate with owner and other doula team members
Marketing	Branding	Complete control	Shared with partner	Done by the group	Complete control	No control
	Website creation	Complete control	Shared with partner(s)	Group control; or already done if joining an existing group	Complete control	No involvement
	Social media, blogging	Complete control	Shared with partner(s)	Shared by group members	Complete control	Not required
	Events, other	Complete control	Shared with partner(s)	Shared by group members	Complete control	May be asked to attend "Meet the Doulas" events or other promos
Control over Reputation		Complete control	Actions of partner(s) reflect on you, for better or worse	Actions of other group members reflect on you, for better or worse	Actions of agency doulas reflect on owner, for better or worse	Can control your own reputation but are associated with the agency brand and overall reputation

Comparison Parameters	Independent Doula	Doula Partnership	Doula Collective	Doula Agency Owner	Agency Doula
Income Potential**	Keep all client fees; occasionally pay for backup	Split the income between the partners	Keep all client fees; may need to pay a fee to collective to cover administrative expenses	Keep percentage of fees	Payment amount pre-determined; agency keeps a percentage; may make it easier for new doulas to earn an income sooner rather than later

* The caveat here is that the business owner must have the skills and determination to stick with it and do what is required to be a successful small business owner.

** The real answer on "income potential" is, "It's up to you!" Each model has its pros and cons and there are many parameters for success.

▥ For more information on doula business models and structures, see Chapter 1 of *The Doula Business Guide, 3rd Edition.*

Examining Your Priorities
Exercise

Take out two different colored highlighters (e.g., yellow and green).
Use the green to highlight any items above that are of value to you or items
that strike you as a strong advantage.
Next, highlight any items in yellow that strike you as a strong disadvantage.
Now, rank the highlighted items according to their importance to you.
A picture should be starting to emerge. Which business model appears to
most happily fit who you are today?

Remember, some of these categories are not mutually exclusive and where you
start out does not necessarily dictate where you end up. You could, for
example, work on building an independent practice as you accept jobs with a
doula agency.

Client Acquisition Process

You have just received an inquiry regarding your doula services. Congratulations! You have succeeded at step one of the process. Now what? Here's a step-by-step overview of the entire process.

Step 1. *Generate leads.* Leads can come from personal contacts, word of mouth, referrals, website traffic, social media contacts, ads, flyers, rack cards, directory listings and more.

Step 2. *Respond to the initial inquiry.* First impressions are super important! Get in the habit of checking your messages daily (whether via Facebook, email or phone). I've secured many jobs because I was the first person to return a call or, even better, answer my phone. There is no doubt that demonstrating availability and responsiveness will work in your favor. Your goals in this initial contact are to build rapport and demonstrate professionalism. You cannot accomplish your goals effectively if your phone message leaves the person questioning whether they have reached the doula, or if your toddler is vying for your attention, or you are otherwise distracted (e.g., driving). If you are unavoidably preoccupied, let callers know that you want to give them your full attention and arrange a better time to call them back.

Have answers to frequently asked questions ready. If you sound unsure or as though you are making it all up on the spot, the client will pick up on your uncertainty and lack of preparedness. Remember, folks seeking doula support may be feeling unsure or anxious. They are seeking guidance, someone they can depend upon. Are you conveying that you will be their Rock of Gibraltar? Some will naturally take the lead on the call, working their way through a set of questions. Others may not really know what to ask or how to interview a doula and will expect you to guide them. Either way, you need to be prepared (though not scripted) with your answers. Spend enough time in this initial call to establish rapport and answer their most pressing questions. I'm going to ballpark it at 15 minutes. More time on the phone is not necessarily better. Some folks will talk and talk if you are willing to indulge them. Others will extract the equivalent of a private childbirth class or advance care planning session over the phone, milking you for information. Do not be afraid to have professional boundaries and help them understand that, once you decide to work together, you have much more in the way of information and resources that you will gladly share. You do not have to give it all away for free now in the hope that they will hire you. Again, they are looking to you for guidance and what you want to guide them to do is to set up an in-person interview with you.

During, or soon after the phone interview, jot down a few notes about the needs of the family, where they live, who the key players are, potential time frame for services and any priorities they shared.

Step 3. *Client interview.* The interview should be set for a mutually convenient time in the near future. Putting them off gives another doula the chance to be first so try and prioritize this. Make it clear that partners and key family members are welcome, even encouraged to participate in the interview since you will all be working together as a team. Your interview success strategies include:

- Be on time.
- Bring your Welcome Packet (see pp. 45–46).
- Review any notes you made after your initial phone call.
- Leave self-doubt, excuses and apologies at home.
- Focus on your top three best doula qualities.
- Take a couple of minutes to ground yourself before stepping out of your car (see p. 105).

At the end of the interview, be very clear about what the next steps are. Presumably, you would like to hear back from them, one way or another, regarding their decision. Let them know if you will hold time for them in your schedule until a specified date or if you book clients on a first-come, first-served basis.

Step 4. *Follow-up.* After the interview, follow up with a short email or a handwritten thank you note. You can affirm that you enjoyed meeting them and welcome the opportunity to be their doula. If there were any special concerns they shared with you, demonstrate your value by providing recommended resources or links for them on those topics. Ask if they thought of any questions they forgot to ask you. And finally, remind them of the approaching deadline (if any).

Step 5. *Seal the deal.* Once the client has chosen to hire you, go ahead and have them sign the contract and pay your non-refundable retainer fee. I don't really consider their spot reserved until they make that first payment, so this is not something to be put off. Birth doulas will want to schedule the first prenatal visit, while postpartum doulas should clarify when they want to be notified that the baby has been born and an anticipated start date for services. For end-of-life doulas, the parameters may vary, depending on how far upstream of hospice care and active dying the person is. Bottom line: If you are going to be "on-call" for clients, you need a retainer fee for that portion of your service regardless of how it plays out (e.g., person dies suddenly before the vigil even begins). Let clients know they are welcome to contact you with any questions or concerns before that first prenatal visit or other doula services begin.

Tracking Client Inquiries

It's helpful to set up a system for tracking initial inquiries from potential clients. Be prepared to give the caller your undivided attention. If this means that you call them back after the kids are in bed or when your partner is available to help, then do that. Clients will appreciate that you care and are professional. Would you want to hire the doula who is interrupted several times as you are speaking with her or the one who is focused on your needs?

If you are just starting out, it is likely you won't have trouble remembering what one or two potential clients share about their past experiences and anticipated needs. But trust me, you will start forgetting the details when five or more folks a month are sharing a variety of concerns, some of them following up with you and some not. Having a form handy where you systematically track this information can help you demonstrate to clients that you are paying attention. She will appreciate not having to remind you that she has a history of postpartum depression, or that her partner is a truck driver who may be out of town when she goes into labor, or that her mother is being transferred home from a rehab facility at the end of the month.

Another benefit of the tracker is that it prompts you to ask how people are finding you and encourages you to systematically track this key information. What are the sources? Knowing the answer to this question identifies the marketing efforts that are working for you (as well as those that may not be worth further investment of time and money). In addition, if the source was a referral, you now know who to thank.

See our sample forms on the next two pages and then adapt, as you see fit, for your business. Are there any other questions you want to ask?

Initial Client Contact Form (Birth/Postpartum Doulas)

Today's Date:

Name:

City:

Phone:

Email Address:

Due Date:

Anticipated Place of Birth:

Care Provider:

1st Baby? What number birth will this be?

VBAC or other information shared about past birth and/or postpartum experiences?

Key Concerns / Motivations:

Questions for Follow-Up / Resources Needed:

Notes:

How did you hear about my services?

Interview Scheduled:

Initial Client Contact Form (End-of-Life Doulas)

Today's Date:

Patient's Name:

Key Decision-Makers/Non-Medical Care Providers:

Living Situation (home or facility)?

City:

Phone:

Email Address:

Diagnosis? Stage of disease?

Under hospice care?

Key Concerns / Motivations:

Questions for Follow-Up / Resources Needed:

Notes:

How did you hear about my services?

Interview Scheduled:

Assembling a Welcome Packet

Once you are ready to start scheduling clients, you should have a handful of Welcome Packets ready to go. Bring your packet along to your interview. When the discussion gets around to your fees and policies, you can bring out the packet and review the information together. Then leave the packet with the couple/family. Many folders have a place inside for holding a business card and you can place your card there. It matters that your packet be professional and attractive.

Purpose of Packet
- Make a positive, professional impression
- Communicate essential information that potential clients can reference
- Establish your brand
- Clarify next steps

Contents
- Welcome letter (on your letterhead; see sample here http://www.inspiredbirthpro.com/heres-your-free-welcome-letter-download/)
- List of services provided
- References
- Client contract
- Favorite article
- What's next? In marketing lingo, this is your "call to action." Spell out precisely what you want the prospective client to do next. For example, you can tell them that you will save time in your schedule for them up to a week after the interview. Walk them through the process.

Tips
- Make your packet visually attractive.
- Have someone proofread everything for flow, clarity and errors.
- Realize that your packet will be a work in progress; you don't need to assemble 20 packets in advance because you are likely to make changes, especially if you are just starting up.
- Infuse your packet with your personality, your brand. It is fine, even desirable, to go online and view samples. Use these to get the ball rolling, a jumping off point. However, it's important to look for ways to stand out and differentiate your business from your competitors, so refrain from merely copying someone else's ideas (plus, the person whose work is being plagiarized probably won't be too happy about it).
- Keep your ideal client in mind as you put your Welcome Packet together (complete the questionnaire on pp. 83–85).
- More is not better. Keep your packet simple, useful. Everything should have a purpose, a reason for being there. If you overload it with articles and resources, then you are: (1) adding to the overall information overload now prevalent in our culture; (2) increasing your costs before the client has committed to you and (3) reducing the chances that the important stuff gets read.

Once you are hired ...

There may be additional resources you want to share with clients and you can provide those at your next visit, including:

- Instructions regarding how and when to contact you when labor begins or, for postpartum doulas, instructions regarding when you want to be contacted after the birth
- Information regarding use of backup and how to access your backup doula(s); or, if you work with a team of doulas, explain how that works
- Client questionnaire, intake form or other tool you have created to elicit clients' expectations and anticipated needs (e.g., birth plan template, advance care planning recommendations); these tools can then be used to guide prenatal discussions or set priorities for postpartum or end-of-life care
- Information you find yourself repeating to every client

Building Value

You may also want to include:

- Favorite community resources. These can also be posted on your website (do a reciprocal links exchange with local providers for the search engine juice while you're at it).
- Free stuff (coupons, samples, etc.)

Keeping your ego intact if you are not hired ...

It's hard not to take it personally, to feel rejected when a couple or family chooses another doula, especially if you enjoyed your time with them and thought things went well during the interview. If you let that feeling rule you, however, you will not last long in this business.

- Shake it off. A very subtle difference between you and another doula may have really resonated with the client. It's not a rejection of you, but rather a choice regarding what's best for them. You cannot be the best fit for everyone; it's just not possible.
- You do not immediately need to change (lower) your fees. Affirm your value with positive self-talk.
- Be curious. Ask yourself whether there is anything you can learn from this loss of a potential client. Anything you can do better going forward? (Sometimes we're just guessing here, but it's worth considering.)
- Truly wish them well in your heart and let it go. Perhaps they will become your customer for a different service you offer (e.g., childbirth classes, placenta encapsulation, home funeral facilitation) or in the future, so keep an open door and a positive attitude.

Forms Checklist

Minimum Requirements
Client contract (Letter of Agreement) _____
Client intake form, questionnaire _____
Your contact information sheet and instructions _____
Invoice _____
Receipt _____
Welcome Packet _____
Calendar(s)
- Big picture (due dates, work flow) _____
- Day-to-day appointments, deadlines _____

Possible Additions
Birth plan template _____
Anticipated postpartum needs of client questionnaire _____
End-of-life planning template _____
Educational topics checklist _____
Recommended resources _____
Any forms or tools you think will be beneficial (list below)

1.
2.
3.
4.

Forms & Tools Resources
- www.InspiredBirthPro.com
- www.MarasWorld.com (See pregnancy planning guides, especially the birth plan template.)
- www.YourDoulaBiz.com
- Do a web search for sample forms.

See *The Doula Business Guide, 3rd Edition* for a discussion on forms and specific guidance regarding your client contract from a risk management perspective (Chapter 7).

Setting Up Your Chart of Accounts in QuickBooks

Think of software such as QuickBooks as an electronic checkbook. This robust piece of software is also capable of generating invoices, receipts, financial statements and more. At a minimum, QuickBooks enables the user to enter income as deposits (tracking who paid you, when, how much and what for) and expenses as debits/checks (tracking vendors you paid, when, how much and what for). Should you ever need written proof of self-employment income (and last year's federal tax form 1040 does not suffice), then you can easily print out a Profit & Loss Statement from QuickBooks.

If you hire an accountant to do your taxes for you each year, he/she can help you with the setup, show you what you need to know, and then be given access to your files when tax time comes around. It's good to involve your accountant at the start so it gets set up in a way that makes sense to them and enables an efficient process.

To learn more about how to use QuickBooks' many features, check out offerings at your local community college or adult learning programs offered through your city's Rec & Ed Department. If you are a do-it-yourself type; the tutorials that come with the program itself are helpful.

To get started, you need to create a Chart of Accounts. Here is a sample Chart of Accounts for a business (mine) offering professional doula trainings and a few products for sale in a rented commercial property. Your list will likely be much shorter than this. Once you have the framework in place (your bookkeeping infrastructure), you simply need to use the system. You can also edit your Chart of Accounts at any time, adding new categories or sub-categories as the need arises or inactivating items that are no longer useful.

To record deposits and debits, transactions are entered into the system assigning each to the appropriate account. You can also create a "class" list to track more detailed information on each transaction if desired. So, for example, when purchasing course pack binders, I can assign that expense as follows: expense category = office supplies; class = end-of-life doula training. At any point in time, I can run a report to see, at a glance, which classes are making a profit, so this level of detail is helpful for my business but may not be needed in yours (and the IRS doesn't require that level of detail).

Income Accounts
- Class revenue
- Consulting fees
- Directory listings *(paid ads on my website)*
- E-Downloads *(online classes, e-books)*
- Miscellaneous income

List **your** anticipated source(s) of income now.

Expense Accounts
- Advertising
- CEU approval *(application fees for contact hour approval)*
- Continuing education *(attendance at conferences, webinars, etc.)*

- Equipment
  - Purchase
  - Rental *(e.g., copier)*
  - Repairs
- Insurance
- Meals/food
- Miscellaneous expense *(parking, gifts, etc.)*
- Miscellaneous fees
  - Bank fees
  - Credit card processing fees
  - Licensing fees
- Occupancy
  - Building maintenance
  - Cleaning services *(Form 1099 may be required)*
  - Communications *(phone, internet)*
  - Rent *(Form 1099 must be filed if you paid the landlord $600 or more per calendar year)*
  - Utilities
- Printing
- Professional affiliations *(certification renewals, membership fees, etc.)*
- Professional services (sub-contractors) *(Form 1099 may be required)*
  - Accountant
  - Graphic design
  - Guest teachers' fees
  - Lawyer
  - Tech support
  - Website design services

Perhaps you might add Backup Doula Services here?

- Supplies
  - Cleaning supplies, paper goods
  - Educational materials
  - Office furnishings
  - Office supplies
  - Postage
  - Software

Or Doula supplies (e.g., books, rebozo, essential oil diffuser) here?

- Travel *(for business purposes)*
  - Lodging
  - Meals *(limit to 50% of cost of meals purchased on the road)*
  - Transportation (air/train/bus fare, airport shuttles, cabs); see pp. 53–55 for mileage tracking when using personal vehicle for business purposes

- Website
  - Hosting
  - Payment gateway
  - Shopping cart

> ## Create your list of anticipated expense categories now.

Cost of Goods Sold Account
- Cost of goods sold*

Equity Account
- Owner's Draw**

Selling inventory is sufficiently complicated to recommend that you consult with an accountant if product sales are part of your business plan. Most small business owners operate on a "cash" basis, but inventory is reported to the IRS on an "accrual" basis, so it is different. Your accountant can ensure that you get it set up right so that you are collecting sales tax as you go and meeting your state's reporting requirements.

**An Owner's Draw account is an equity account in which QuickBooks tracks withdrawals of a company's assets to pay an owner. When you write yourself a paycheck, you classify it as an Owner's Draw. It will register as a debit in the checking account, however it will not register as an "expense" on a Profit & Loss report. This is helpful because your Profit & Loss report will reflect your total gross income minus your business expenses. The net amount should equal the total amount of Owner's Draws plus any remaining excess not withdrawn for personal use. At the end of the tax year, the net amount is what you will owe taxes on whether you removed the funds from business checking for personal use or not.*

Staying Out of Trouble with the IRS—Startup Exercises

Exercise 1 (30 minutes)

Go to www.IRS.gov and print out the following forms for the most recent tax year:

- Form 1040 Individual Income Tax Return
- Schedule C Profit or Loss from Business
- Schedule SE Self-Employment Tax
- Form 1099-Misc and Form 1096 Annual Summary and Transmittal of U.S. Information Returns *(required if you anticipate paying a contract worker, such as your backup doula or website designer, at least $600 in the current tax year)*
- Form 8829 *(if you plan to claim a deduction for business use of your home OR you can use the Simplified Method directly from Schedule C)*

There may be additional forms that you will need, such as a special form to calculate depreciation on an equipment purchase, but this will become obvious as you work your way through the Schedule C.

Spend a few minutes reviewing these forms, just to become a bit familiar. If this is not your area of strength, it is fine to turn everything over to your accountant, but you still need to provide the basic information that your accountant needs. And the more organized you are, the less you will have to pay your accountant. This exercise will help you understand how the IRS expects to receive your information. For example, to take a mileage deduction for use of your personal vehicle for business purposes, review the required documentation on page two of Schedule C.

To substantiate a deduction of $1,000 for website design services or $850 in backup doula services, you will need to send payees a Form 1099-Misc by January 31 of the new tax year. The corresponding Form 1096—a summary of all the 1099s filed—then gets sent directly to the IRS. The information needed to complete the form includes: each payee's legal name as it appears on their taxes, their address and social security number if a sole proprietor, or employer identification number (EIN; aka FIN or federal identification number) if they are incorporated. It's best to collect this information at the time services are rendered rather than scrambling to track down the person (or potential tax dodger) after the fact.

Additional Deductions

There are a few deductions you may be eligible for that likely will *not* be reflected in your Profit & Loss Statement of as-you-go income and expenses. These are typically calculated once per year, as part of figuring your annual income tax return and are considered below.

- **Home office.** You may qualify for a deduction for business use of your home. The area in question must be used exclusively for business purposes and is calculated as a percentage of the overall square footage of your home or apartment. This percentage is then applied to your total monthly rent paid or annual mortgage interest paid. From there, the IRS has some other calculations necessary to arrive at the deduction amount (see Form 8829). The deduction can include utilities and repairs as well, applying the same percentage, so be sure and save those bills/receipts, along with your other business-related receipts. You can also opt to use the Simplified Method for calculating this deduction rather than the Form 8829 (see the instructions for Schedule C).

- **Internet access.** On my sample Chart of Accounts (see pp. 48–50), I included internet access as part of my overall occupancy costs for rental of a business property. In this situation, 100% of my internet bill at the office is deductible and it shows as a monthly expense in QuickBooks. However, if you are only working from home, then you will be paying your family's internet bill from your personal checking. In this case, to claim the deduction, you will need to make your best reasonable guess regarding the percentage of your home internet bill that reflects use for business purposes. Be sure and save these bills as well, along with your other tax receipts.

- **Phone.** A dedicated business line is 100% deductible. Most cell phone users, however, use their phone for multiple purposes and plan share with other family members. Only claim a reasonable percentage for business use on *your* phone (clearly not 100%).

- **Depreciation.** Check with your accountant if you invest in equipment for your business (e.g., a copier, computer, printer, video camera, etc.). You can claim a deduction for depreciation on this investment (use Form 4562 Depreciation and Amortization).

- **Mileage.** The IRS requires written proof, preferably a log, of mileage claimed. To figure the deduction, an annual per mile rate is set by the IRS (just google it to see what the current rate is). On occasion, the IRS resets the rate during the year (based on dramatic fluctuations in the cost of gas), so it is helpful to track the associated travel dates as well. I recall one year when there was one rate for the months January through July and then a different rate for the remaining months in the year.

Exercise 2

1. Explore systems for tracking your mileage. Possibilities include:
   - Phone apps (e.g., MileIQ.com)
   - Mileage tracker booklet purchased at an office supply store and kept in your car
   - Use MapQuest (or similar app) to determine number of miles to and from clients' homes, the hospital, meetings, work-related errands, etc. Then use your work calendar/client records to determine total number of trips.

2. Which reporting system are you most likely to use? If you can never remember to note your mileage into a phone app or booklet, then you really don't have a system. In that case, perhaps MapQuest is the way to go. Even so, it will be useful if you have a form where you do the calculations for each client, perhaps at the end of services (see samples following).

3. Set up your system and enter all your mileage for year to date.

Birth Doula Mileage Worksheet
(Using MapQuest)

Client's Name	Address	Distance from home to client	Number of round trips	Distance from home to hospital	Number of round trips	Total mileage

Postpartum/End-of-Life Doula Mileage Worksheet
(Using MapQuest)

Client's Name	Address	Distance from home to client	Number of round trips	Client errands – additional miles	Total mileage

Mileage Log
(Track as you go)

Odometer mileage at beginning of the current tax year (or when car was first placed in service for business purposes): _____

Date	Purpose	Starting Mileage	Ending Mileage	Total

Odometer mileage at end of the current tax year: _____

Bookkeeping System Checklist

Set up system to track: **Done**
- Income   _____
- Expenses   _____
- Mileage   _____

Set up filing system for storing:
- Receipts for all purchases; invoices from vendors   _____
- Monthly bank statements (both personal checking and business checking)   _____
- Home utility bills (if claiming deduction for home office)   _____
- Home repair bills (if claiming deduction for home office)   _____
- Cell phone bills, internet bills   _____
- Your annual business calendar   _____
- Client records   _____

Storage Requirements ~ Keep it all for seven years
I keep everything in my file cabinet until the end of the year. Then I pull it all, set it aside for tax season and create new folders for the current tax year. Once my taxes have been filed with the government for the most recent tax year, I store all the receipts and documents together in a large box, marked with the tax year, in my basement. Keep all documentation for a period of seven years. As you add a new box each year, you can shred/recycle the stuff that is now eight years old.

Infrastructure Summary Checklist

TASKS	✔
Choose a business name	
Purchase your URL	
Reserve your Facebook business page	
Protect your name (DBA or incorporate)	
Formalize business model (e.g., incorporate, complete partnership agreement)	
List services provided	
Set your fees, terms of payment, refund policy	
Create policy regarding use of backup doula(s)	
Set limit on your travel radius (How far are you willing to travel to serve?)	
Decide where you will meet with clients	
Create your business forms, paperwork	
Set up a bookkeeping system	
Set up a filing and storage system for receipts, etc.	
Establish a mileage tracking system	
Open business checking account (LLC owners)	
Add DBA to personal checking account (sole proprietors using business name)	
Get set up to accept electronic payments	
Purchase liability insurance (if desired)	

If you need further guidance regarding considerations associated with these tasks, see *The Doula Business Guide, 3rd Edition.*

Part 3

Plan

Goals and Activities Business Planner

It can feel daunting to be at the beginning of a large project. When you get up on a Monday morning and your "to do" list is, essentially, "Everything," who wouldn't want to crawl back under the covers? Would it feel less overwhelming to have "Everything" broken down into bite-size pieces? Suppose you could consult your prioritized task list and choose one you are in the mood to tackle (or cross off the list!) each day.

Your plan is a bit like putting together a jigsaw puzzle. There are lots of small pieces. Think through the details of how to get where you want to be. The timeframe and pace of your work are up to you and will likely be dictated by a variety of factors. No one creates a business overnight. It takes intent, time and focus.

Here's a Sample Plan

Goal #1. Launch my birth doula business. (January 2020)

Objective A. Complete professional certification process. (Deadline)

    Activity 1. Purchase certification materials. (Deadline)

    Activity 2. Complete reading requirements. (Deadline)

    Activity 3. Continue to list out the certification requirements (and deadlines!) ....

Objective B. Develop paperwork. (Deadline)

    Activity 1. Create a client contract. (Deadline)

    Activity 2. Write up instructions for how to best contact me when services are needed. (Deadline)

    Activity 3. Determine what other paperwork will facilitate delivery of services and communication with clients (e.g., a Welcome Packet; see p. 45). (Deadline)

Objective C. Pull together a starter "birth bag." (Deadline)

    Activity 1. Make a list of items I want to have on hand when at a birth, including items for self-care. (Deadline)

    Activity 2. Explore sources and prices for items that must be purchased. (Deadline)

    Activity 3. Prioritize list according to need/require/desire (see Budget Worksheet p. 70). (Deadline)

Goal #2. Develop professional connections in my birthing community. (Ongoing)

Objective A. Identify a minimum of three potential back-up doulas. (Deadline)

      Activities List: How will you do this?

Objective B. Attend three networking events this year. (Deadline)

      Activities List: Are you aware of appropriate annual events/venues or do you need to research this? (Deadline)

Goal #3. Launch a website. (Deadline date)

What will it take to get this done?

Comments

The activities listed above can be further broken down, with several tasks listed. For example, to read the required books for certification, you first must procure them. Perhaps you don't want to just go on Amazon and buy them all and, preferring to stretch a dollar, you decide to ask your local library to get copies through the inter-library loan system.

It can be good to have more than one goal you are working on. Perhaps you just can't stand the thought of working on the client contract today, but it would be okay to do some doula time on Facebook, read a required book or play with creating a list of things to take with you on the job. Two or three different goals will give you a bit more flexibility in how you approach your work and you'll still be able to systematically cross items off your list! On any given day, your creative juices might not be especially flowing but ordering your books may feel doable.

You may also want to attach a budget to the purchase items on your list, as finances are often a limiting factor for start-up business owners. These items can later be ranked in order of importance using our Budget Worksheet (see p. 70).

Your time budget needs consideration as well. Make your best guess regarding how much time you imagine each objective/activity will take and measure this against your overall goal. Later, as you assess your progress toward goals, these guesses may provide a clue to what is going on if you are routinely under-performing. Finally, you can use our Time Tracker Tool (see pp. 78–79) to track hours spent working on your business for a little more insight.

On the following pages you will find a Goal Setting Template. Use this to set some goals and organize associated tasks. Review your progress at the end of each week, month, year. Were your goals realistic? What are your successes? Where do you feel stuck? What steps can you take to get "unstuck"?

> You are the captain of your own ship.
> You need to set a destination and chart your course.

GOAL: _____

Objective	Activities	By when? / Est. hours
1.		
	1.	
	2.	
	3.	
	4.	
	5.	
2.		
	1.	
	2.	
	3.	
	4.	
	5.	
3.		
	1.	
	2.	
	3.	
	4.	
	5.	
4.		
	1.	
	2.	
	3.	
	4.	
	5.	

GOAL: _____

Objective	Activities	By when? / Est. hours
1.		
	1.	
	2.	
	3.	
	4.	
	5.	
2.		
	1.	
	2.	
	3.	
	4.	
	5.	
3.		
	1.	
	2.	
	3.	
	4.	
	5.	
4.		
	1.	
	2.	
	3.	
	4.	
	5.	

GOAL: _____

Objective	Activities	By when? / Est. hours
1.		
	1.	
	2.	
	3.	
	4.	
	5.	
2.		
	1.	
	2.	
	3.	
	4.	
	5.	
3.		
	1.	
	2.	
	3.	
	4.	
	5.	
4.		
	1.	
	2.	
	3.	
	4.	
	5.	

Create a Budget for Your Business

It's easy to get distracted when it comes to spending money. We become seduced by the lovely office space, pretty rebozo, latest book recommendation or advertising opportunity and end up making impulse decisions. Unless you are well-off and can indulge your whims, then lack of discipline in this area will get in the way of your success. Some financial planning is required.

What are the start-up costs for a doula business? These will vary depending on which professional doula organization you affiliate with and your geographic location. For example, California residents will pay significantly more to incorporate as a limited liability corporation than residents of other states. Do your research and fill in the numbers below.

Start-Up Costs

Item	Comments	Cost
Training	Check to ensure you have included all the training requirements.	
Travel expenses associated with training	If any; include cost of lodging, transportation and 50 percent of meals on the road	
Certification and membership fees	What is the full cost here?	
Incorporation in your state	Not relevant if you plan to be a sole proprietor	
Reserve your domain name	May want more than one variation (e.g., dot.com, dot.net and dot.org)	
Books	Many of these can be borrowed from the library or purchased used. Consider which ones you need to own for reference purposes versus ones you need to read once for certification.	

Item	Comments	Cost
Birth doula supplies • Carrying bag • Personal care items • Birth ball, washable cover, carrying strap • Rebozo • Rice sock • Massage lotion, tools • Reference book(s) *(Labor Progress Handbook* recommended) • Honey sticks, lip balm, combs, etc. • Other?	You may not truly "need" any of the items on your list. Decide on your priorities.	
Postpartum doula supplies • Carrying bag • Personal care items • Reference book (LLL's *Breastfeeding Answer Book—Pocket Guide* recommended) • A couple of baby carriers • Other?	Not a lot needed here; may not even need much in the way of personal care. Carriers can be picked up used at yard sales. Decide on your priorities.	
End-of-life doula supplies • Carrying bag • Personal care items • Book(s) with visualization scripts, meditations, prayers, etc. • Aromatherapy diffuser and essential oils • Other?	Not a lot needed here; may not even need much in the way of personal care, unless you are vigiling. Decide on your priorities.	
Professional liability insurance	Not required; this is a personal decision each doula needs to make.	

Item	Comments	Cost
Home office set-up • Computer • Printer • File cabinet • Bookshelf • Office supplies (paper, file folders, etc.) • Accounting software or ledger book • Other?	Prioritize. Look for used furnishings. Your needs could become a bit more elaborate if you are setting up a space for meeting with clients, teaching classes, etc.	
Website • Hosting • Design services	Some folks start with a do-it-yourself template website. The limitations of this approach will manifest eventually, but it is better than nothing and you can always upgrade once you are making the income to cover it.	
Marketing materials • Business cards • Rack cards	You can use design templates available online or, if your skills aren't up to it, hire a graphic designer to give you a professional look.	
Other priority items	Are there other things that you absolutely must prioritize or everything else is moot? A car repair? Child care?	

For more information about the advisability of incorporating, purchasing professional liability insurance, choosing between a simple template or custom-designed website, or any other item on the list, see *The Doula Business Guide, 3rd Edition.*

Ongoing Costs

There will always be a cost of doing business. Successful business owners invest in their businesses and are always seeking the best return on their investment (ROI) available.

Marketing

What is a customer worth to you? The ROI is an essential piece of the equation when it comes to budgeting for your business. Will purchasing a business-card size ad in the local monthly natural health publication pay off? Who knows? It's a gamble. However, if you track how each client inquiring about services found you, then you will be able to do the calculation and make more informed decisions going forward.

$$\text{Cost of ad} \div \text{Number of leads generated} = \text{Cost of customer acquisition}$$

The next part of the calculation is to define how much money your average customer pays you and plug that into a new equation to determine whether your investment paid off. For example:

$$\$900 \text{ (average income per customer)}$$
$$- \$40 \text{ (cost of customer acquisition)}$$
$$= \$860 \text{ profit}$$

In the example above, is the lead worth an out-of-pocket investment of $40? Probably yes. But if your average customer pays you $300, then the ROI is not so great.

Professional Affiliation

Membership fees, re-certification fees and the cost of continuing education are ongoing expenses for doula business owners.

Business Expansion

Many business owners diversify over time, adding new products or services, acting on new trends, market opportunities and so on. At some point, your business may outgrow your home, rendering it untenable to continue in that location and making the allure of your own office space or dream of a center more compelling. Expansion may involve acquiring new skills, usually introduces new risks, and always involves an investment of time and money. Careful planning is in order.

Need ~ Require ~ Desire

I introduce this sorting principle in *The Doula Business Guide*. Briefly summarizing here, items on the "need" list are essential to the work you are doing. You cannot be a doula without basic training and reliable transportation, for example. "Require" represents the next level of priority. One requires a bag of self-care items, a website and perhaps an especially helpful reference book. What else do you require to be successful? Finally, items on the "desire" list are the things you simply want. It might be interesting to note how long an item remains on your "desire" list as an indication of its value to your business. On the following page, I have provided a chart for prioritizing and planning your purchases. Be sure and work your way through the "needs" first.

Budget Worksheet

NEED	Budgeted Amount	By When?

REQUIRE	Budgeted Amount	By When?

DESIRE	Budgeted Amount	By When?

"Pie of Time" Exercise

Where does the time go? Where indeed? When my second child was five months old, I was feeling frustrated about not getting work done. At the time, I was still running my bill-paying word processing and editing business while pursuing my new career as a childbirth educator, doula and midwife. I honestly could not understand why I could only manage to fit in one or two hours per day on data entry when I previously was able to do much more, so I decided to track my time. It turns out I spent five hours per day breastfeeding! Three more hours were taken up with other infant care-related tasks including laundry and playing with my baby or going for walks with him. That year, an hour and a half each weekday involved transporting my other son to school and back (during which times the baby invariably took his unfortunately short naps). And so it goes. After three days of charting, I was no longer wondering where the time goes. Clearly, being a mom of two that year was a full-time job!

How do you spend your day?

1. **Track it.** You probably think you have a pretty good sense of it, but there is nothing quite like tracking your time for a few days on paper. Then you can really see the patterns and there is no room for self-deception. The key is to not make any conscious changes quite yet. If you watch TV for four hours, write it down. If you shop online for an hour, write it down. Be honest. Fill in your "pie of time" on the next page, using the full 24-hour cycle. Now you know where your time goes.

2. **Consider your results.** You may not have realized before that your quick Facebook "check-ins" routinely turn into 50 minutes. Or that watching your favorite show on television regularly becomes three hours of mindless channel surfing. Which of your existing habits and patterns are serving you well? Which are not enhancing your life? Which are non-negotiable? Anything superfluous?

3. **What does your ideal "pie of time" look like?** Next fill in what your ideal "pie of time" looks like. What is the minimum number of hours of sleep you require to feel good? What time of day are you naturally more productive? How much time should be allotted for relaxation? Have you budgeted any time for self-care? For working *on* your business?

4. **Reconcile your pies (the real versus the ideal).** Where are the discrepancies between your actual rhythms and how you choose to spend your day versus your ideal timetable? Following are some questions for consideration (continued p. 75):

Current "Pie of Time"

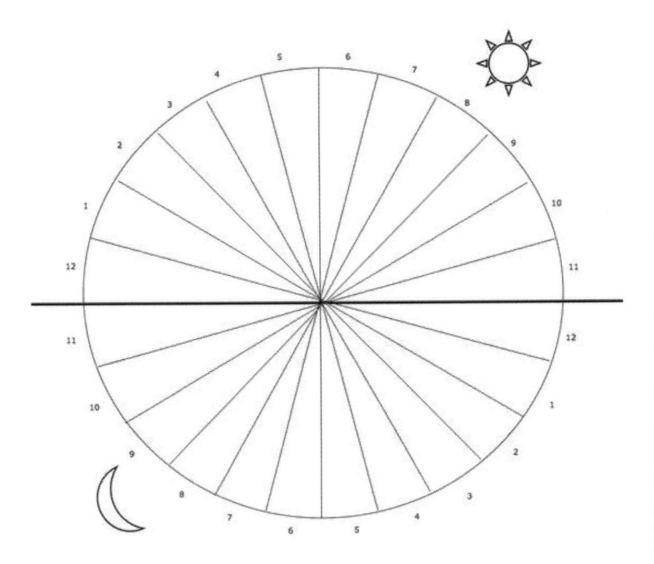

Ideal "Pie of Time"

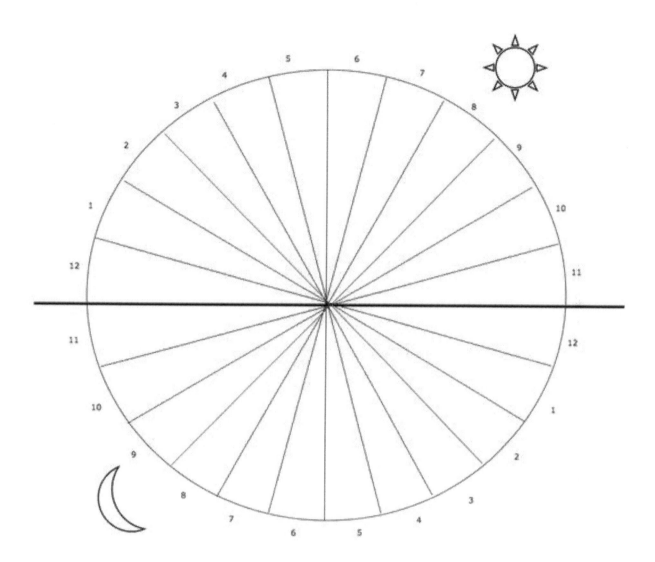

Reconciliation "Pie of Time"

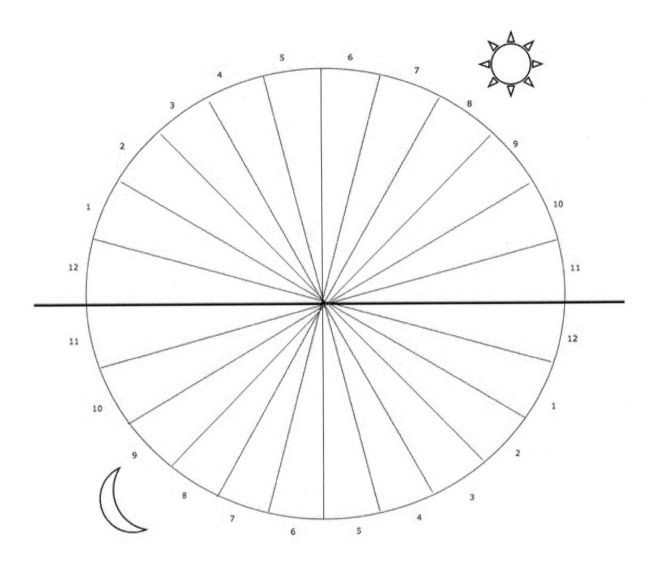

- What are your priority activities and how much time do these require?

- Are you trying to do too much? Can something go off the list that you would not miss?

- Can your kids or partner help more? (Get the family involved in problem-solving this one.)

- If you could change one habit to be more productive, what would it be?

- Where can you find that extra hour or two a few times a week to focus on developing your business and reaching your career goals?

Time Management Strategies

- Know how you spend your time (see "Pie of Time" Exercise on pp. 71–75).

- Identify your priorities.

- Use a planning tool to generate a "to-do" list (see our Goals and Activities Business Planner on pp. 61–65).

- Get organized. Declutter and implement a system for handling information (see pp. 29–31).

- Try time blocking. Take a high priority item from your "to do" list and assign a specific block of time to work on it. During that time, minimize interruptions and focus solely on the task at hand. Do not check email, surf the web, look at text messages or answer the phone. Just because someone else has decided to contact you (or hijack your agenda), does not mean you have to respond on their time frame (now). One expert recommends a four-hour block of time (including a fifteen-minute break in the middle) to maximize concentration and achievement. This feels just right to me.

- Become more disciplined when using social media. Be clear whether you are enjoying recreational time or engaging for business purposes. If the latter, be purposeful and set a timer.

- Use the Time Tracker tool (p. 78) to help determine your most productive time of day, especially when mental focus is required.

Multi-tasking

- Use the voice recorder app on your phone to capture everything from fabulous ideas to items for your "to do" list when you are out and about, driving, etc.

- Listen to educational programs or books on tape while driving. Need to learn more about marketing? Gather some audio resources to multi-task your drive time.

On a personal level …

- Perhaps your needs and the kids' needs can dovetail? For example, a family karate class that gets them away from their screens and discharges some of that abundant energy while you get a workout and make new friends is a win/win.

- Limit the amount of time you spend schlepping kids about. Perhaps limiting extra-curricular activities to two per child is enough, given the needs of all family members? How about ride sharing?

- Just say "no" when asked to do something you don't want to do. I'm not saying to not help a friend or family member when they need it, but you don't have to say "yes" every time someone imposes on you (your kids' school, church, favorite political cause or nonprofit group). It's not forever …

- If tempted to add one more thing to the to-do list when you are already desperately juggling multiple balls, think "What are my priorities?" Consider which balls are going to get dropped if you say "yes" and then make a conscious choice.

- Cutting out sleep to get it all done is not an option. Occasionally you can get by without your required minimum but cutting needed hours of sleep is unsustainable. The effects of sleep deprivation are cumulative and will take their toll.

Time Tracker

Month: _____ **Week 1**

Day	Monday	Tuesday	Wednesday	Thursday	Friday	Saturday	Sunday
Time Working							
Total Hours							

Month: _____ **Week 2**

Day	Monday	Tuesday	Wednesday	Thursday	Friday	Saturday	Sunday
Time Working							
Total Hours							

Month: _____ **Week 3**

Day	Monday	Tuesday	Wednesday	Thursday	Friday	Saturday	Sunday
Time Working							
Total Hours							

Month: _____   **Week 4**

Day	Monday	Tuesday	Wednesday	Thursday	Friday	Saturday	Sunday
Time Working							
Total Hours							

Month: _____   **Week 5**

Day	Monday	Tuesday	Wednesday	Thursday	Friday	Saturday	Sunday
Time Working							
Total Hours							

The One-Page Business Plan

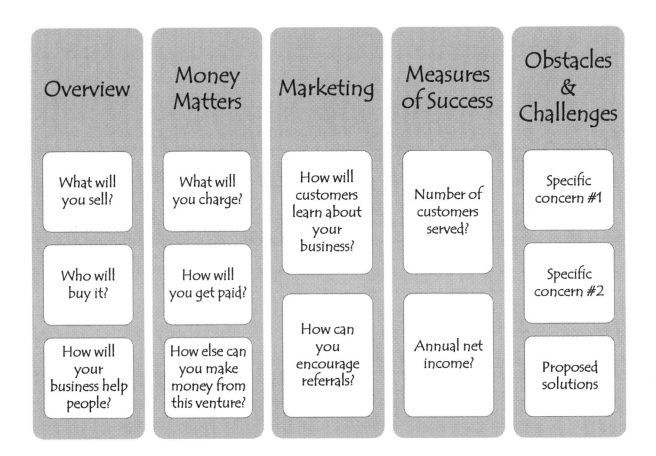

Overview	Money Matters	Marketing	Measures of Success	Obstacles & Challenges
What will you sell?	What will you charge?	How will customers learn about your business?	Number of customers served?	Specific concern #1
Who will buy it?	How will you get paid?	How can you encourage referrals?	Annual net income?	Specific concern #2
How will your business help people?	How else can you make money from this venture?			Proposed solutions

Exercise

Briefly answer each question across the five categories. One or two sentences should suffice. Everything here is important. Keep tweaking your answers as your business develops and revisit the plan periodically. For example, your obstacles and challenges may change significantly, depending on market forces and a variety of factors outside of your control.

Part 4

Grow

Your Ideal Customer Questionnaire

No one can be the right doula match for every client. Think about the top five qualities you would most value in choosing a doula for yourself. What about the top five traits or behaviors that you would most want to steer clear of? Here's mine:

Yes Please	No Thank You
Nonjudgmental	Judgmental
Sense of humor	Earnest
Calm demeanor	Nervous energy, talkative, drama
Graceful, self-aware	Self-centered, unaware of needs of others
Resourceful	Lame excuses

For me, the experience level and knowledge base of the doula are not top priorities. I'm more concerned with who she is and what her overall energy or vibe feels like. I don't particularly care whether she is a mother herself, but I suspect that if she is a mom, her humor may be more likely to sync with mine. I'm not looking for knowledge, tons of experience and a bag of tricks. I don't feel I need that because my belief is I can do this. I just want support and I want to laugh. I want to give my husband permission to come and go as he pleases and I don't want my doula (or anyone else) judging him for his choice. And, while there is nothing inherently wrong with being earnest, it's not the right balance for me since I have my own tendencies in that direction. I could go on, but I think you can see how personal this is.

The more clarity you can come to regarding your "best match," the better you can position yourself in the marketplace by crafting meaningful messages that resonate with your ideal customer. You can also steer away from those folks who would likely be better served by another (different) doula. Non-congruent expectations can too easily turn into trouble and are best avoided. The whole relationship can be a struggle and, in the end, everyone is left with a bad taste in their mouth. This is not the way to build a good referral network for your business! Take some time to consider your answers to the following questions.

- What problems do you solve for the people you serve?

- Brainstorm characteristics of the types of people who are most likely to be experiencing the problems listed above.

  o   Where do they live?

  o   What is their income bracket?

  o   What is their gender, age, marital status?

  o   What do they care about?

  o   Where do they spend their time?

  o   Where do they spend their time online?

- Who will gain the most from what you have to offer (the problems you are solving)? Who has the most to lose from not being proactive about these problems?

- With whom do you most want to work? What is most important to you? Are there particular market segments that stand out, such as location, condition or income bracket?

- What expertise do you have? Do you have a niche specialty (see p. 106)?

- Are there certain types of people or market segments who will be your perfect match?

- Who else is serving the same clientele in your market?

- What are you doing differently, better than the competition? Why are you uniquely qualified to solve the problem(s) listed under #1 above?

- What is your vibe? Think of two or three words that describe your energy and what you are known for.

Summary

A picture of your ideal client should be emerging. Can you see her/him/them in your mind's eye? Now you are ready to begin crafting a message that speaks to this person, one that she/he will feel drawn to and resonate with. Keep the vision of your ideal customer front of mind as you develop your business. Your prototype will inform the tone, language, feel and content of your website, even the colors you choose.

For a couple of years, I had a pink office where my partner and I met with our clients. Pink with darker pink trim. The color was chosen to complement a rug that we both liked. Remarkably, several clients spontaneously reported feeling "calm" when they were in the space. An exploration into color theory reveals that pink represents caring, compassion, love and understanding and is associated with giving and receiving care. We did not intentionally create this effect for our clients; it was serendipitous. But you *can* use color intentionally as you build your unique brand.

Resources

The Voice Bureau: Brand Voice Development for Values-Based Business
www.thevoicebureau.com
Take the assessment on *The 16 Voice Values in Action and What They Think, Do and Say.* The results will help you gain insight into why certain people are drawn to you and what you should watch out for as you grow your brand.

The Meaning of Color
www.color-meanings.com

Professional Networking Worksheet

My Top 5 Most Desirable Contacts …

Who in your community can send you referrals? Identify your top five most desirable source of referrals (the persons/practices/businesses who are best positioned to send you your ideal customers)? Brainstorm the power players.

1.

2.

3.

4.

5.

Next Steps

- Fill in contact information for the folks on your list.
- Learn more about them (e.g., read their websites).
- Consider your strategy for making contact.
- Do it!
- Cultivate the relationship(s)—ongoing.

Outreach Events/Venues Worksheet

Be on the lookout for Outreach Events that might be a good fit for you and your services. Can you be an exhibitor or participate in some way?

- Community Health Fair, Baby Fair, Green Fair (EOLDs can provide info on green burial), Seniors Fair
- Women's Expos, Infant/Toddler Expos
- Alternative Health Care Provider gatherings
- Professional conferences (e.g., midwives, doulas, hospice and palliative care professionals, advance care planning, etc.)
- Other?

Brainstorm venues where you can potentially reach your ideal customers and make a short presentation on doulas or a related topic.

- College classes, including your local community colleges and adult education programs (e.g., early childhood development class; nursing students; women's studies; medical student clubs; gerontology students; anything to do with aging, hospice, palliative care; and so on)
- Whole Foods lecture/demonstration series (e.g., a postpartum doula might propose a presentation on introducing solid foods; a birth doula might speak on herbs and super foods high in calcium and iron; or an end-of-life doula might offer to present on the role of aromatherapy or flower essences in palliative care).
- Local library speaker series
- Other?

Get in the Information Flow

Start by picking up freebie newsletters and local papers and make note of events listings. Subscribe to e-newsletters by key doula industry leaders. In addition to their own self-promotion, these can keep you in the loop regarding local, regional, national and international conferences and events of interest as well as latest developments in the field. And, of course, Facebook groups are a great way to stay current with upcoming events and opportunities.

Event Planning Guide

You will need at least 3–6 months to properly promote an event you are hosting. In some cases, for example, joining an educational series that someone else is hosting, you might simply let your host do the bulk of the promotion for you. Still, if something is worth your time at all, then why not do what you can to generate interest?

1. **Name your event.** The name should pique interest among your target audience. What's in it for them? How do you solve a problem they have or meet an unmet need?

2. **Schedule your event.** There can be a fair amount of guess work here but don't miss the obvious, such as avoiding scheduling a Health Fair at the same time as the local college's big-time football game. Or on Mother's Day or in the middle of Spring Break.

3. **Set the location.** Find an appropriate space in a central location with ample free parking. If renting space, check whether the host organization offers any help with promoting your event. If there is good crossover in your audiences, this can work well.

4. **Participate in someone else's event.** When reserving exhibitor space as part of a larger event that someone else is planning, see what is involved with becoming an exhibitor and read all the rules.

   - Do not make assumptions that electricity will be available, that there will be a wall behind your display area available for your use or that it is permissible to share a table with another business. Can you sell merchandise? Is a tablecloth provided or should you bring one?
   - Note what the refund policy is if you are required to make a deposit up front so that you can determine the level of risk you are assuming.
   - Be sure you know who the target audience is for the event. Is it low-income families? Teen mothers? Middle-to-upper-income families in their childbearing years? Folks interested in natural health? Professionals? Consumers? Which one gives you the most bang for your buck or has the most cross-over with your business?

If the price of an exhibit table seems high, a better strategy might be to attend the event as a member of the public and assess whether you think exposure in such a venue would pay off for your business in the future. If so, now you can plan and budget for next year. I have paid $100 for a table (and given up a Saturday) in a venue where there were more vendors than visitors to the event because the organizers didn't know what they were doing and failed to promote it properly. A successful track record of holding an annual event is more likely to yield a higher return for the vendor. Also, consider that two or four doulas might split the cost of renting a table (if allowed) and together create more buzz than someone going solo. Plus, it's more fun!

5. **Identify what help you might need.** It is grueling to "woman" an exhibitor's table through a full-day conference or trade show. Part of the benefit of participating in these events is not just exposure to the folks who attend, but the networking connections you can make among fellow exhibitors. You will need someone to hold down the fort so you can make the rounds, get a bite to eat, attend an educational session and so on. In some venues, organizers might also be featuring short educational sessions—perhaps you could sign up to be a presenter? On the other hand, if you are simply hosting your own event, you will still likely benefit from having a helper who can facilitate hosting duties such as getting folks to sign in, replenishing the tea supply, greeting late-comers and so on.

6. **Design your exhibit.** You will need a sign. A banner can work IF there is a wall to hang it on behind your table or you have a way to attach it to the front of your table. The tri-fold displays that sit on the table might seem like a good idea. These items cost over $300, come with a carrying case, and are not worth half the money in my opinion. The folding mechanism breaks easily. Plus, once the display is set up, you can no longer sit *behind* your table. You will need to sit or stand next to it (if there is space) or in front of it (if there is not). This is awkward. A vertical banner with a portable stand is a viable alternative. You can have this designed by a local graphic artist/printer or go online to an outlet like VistaPrint. This investment should serve your business well for years to come. How else can you make your table attractive and engaging? What are others doing to create visual interest and draw folks in?

7. **Engage your audience.** Think "how can I maximize this opportunity to create buzz about my business"? Be creative here and have fun with it. For example, we have featured a "Make Your Own Rice Sock" display for visitors to our exhibit table. It's a relatively inexpensive way to go—cheap bags of cotton tube socks, bulk white rice and a pound of lavender with a large bowl to catch any spillage. Design a pretty flyer with instructions for use as a standard first aid and comfort item. Don't forget to put your business name, phone number and website URL on the instructions. This one works because it draws people to the exhibit and engages them. You could do the same with a chair massage or a birth ball demo. Raffle off a gift item or free class. Have a chocolate give-away or two. You get the idea …

8. **Use local media to promote your event.**

   - Compile a list of local media outlets, noting which ones have calendar sections that might list your event. Pick up all those freebie magazines from their various distribution points in stores, coffee houses, waiting rooms, etc. Identify media that target families, the elderly, or are health focused. Note deadlines for submission to get your event posted (this can sometimes be as short as a couple of weeks in advance or longer depending on the publication). Some publications might charge a small amount ($10–20) for a calendar listing—a relatively inexpensive ad.
   - Update your media list annually.
   - Don't neglect radio, television and online media in your efforts.
   - Send out a Press Release to the radio and TV media folks via email. It works best if you are targeting the *current editor* of the department or feature column with

which your business is most closely aligned. These folks are always looking for material. By keeping yourself in front of them, you have self-identified as an expert in your field. They may end up calling you for an article or interview down the road. Marketing is about making connections with people.

9. **Think ahead.** Collect names and emails of folks who visit your table by inviting them to sign up for your e-newsletter or some other incentive. Email addresses are an asset for your business. On the other hand, do not take emails off the Exhibitor List and simply add them to your list. This is spamming.

10. **Promote your event widely.**

   - Design a flyer and display/distribute it.
   - Send out notices to everyone on your email list.
   - Use social media to create a buzz. An event page with an RSVP component on Facebook is good. Share widely in the groups that allow some promotional stuff. And ask your "friends" to share as well.
   - Brainstorm other ways of reaching your target audience.

11. **Make it systematic.** The first time you do an event, there is a lot of work involved. However, when it is time to do another one, it should be a great deal easier. The key is to keep a record of what you are doing and when. Something as simple as a list of what to bring with you to the event should be saved. If the process is documented, then it will be easier to integrate help at some point in the future. If your system is everything is in your head, then you do not have a system.

12. **Have fun!**

Understanding Keywords

> ## SEO or Search Engine Optimization =
>
> the process of affecting the visibility of a website or a web page
> in a search engine's unpaid or "organic" results
>
> ## Keyword =
>
> word or phrase used by the search engines to find a relevant web page

What words or phrases are future customers likely to enter when searching online for your services? These are your keywords. Keywords are an essential component of SEO. Strategic use of keywords, embedded in your content, will result in increased traffic to your website. The more people who come to your website, the better your Google ranking. Since most online searchers do not look past the first page of results in Google, your goal is to be among the top ten listings. Approximately one third of the traffic generated from a search will go to the website listed first in the results, so the closer to the top you can get, the better.

Keyword Tips:

- Each page on your website should be optimized for the keywords you want to highlight on that page.

- Each blog post should highlight specific keywords. Be intentional.

- Google tends to ignore "stop words" in keyword phrases (e.g., the, a, and, in) so it may be best to avoid these if possible. (I have struggled with this for my end-of-life doula training business because "of" is part of the keyword phrase; since the phrase doesn't read well without the "of," I have chosen to leave it in.)

- Location is important for doulas and many other service providers. Consider incorporating your location in your keywords (e.g., Ann Arbor doulas, birth doula Boston, postpartum doula Miami and so on). At a minimum, ensure that your location and area served are visible to the search engines on your homepage and elsewhere throughout your site.

- For some help, check out the Google AdWords Keyword Planner—a free tool that allows you to research how families are using the internet when searching for what you have to offer. You can learn how often a keyword is used in your area. Even more useful, you will see variations on the keyword that may not have occurred to you. You do not need to start building an AdWords account (paid advertising and a complex process) to use this tool—just play a bit.

- If you're not a fan of the Keyword Planner tool, try doing a search on one of your focus keywords. At the bottom of the results page, you will see "Searches related to [the keywords you entered]." This will give you some of the variations on how folks are searching.

Brainstorming Exercise

Are you ready to generate your most relevant keywords? Here are a few terms to get you started. What variations might searchers use? (Brainstorm your answers and then play with Google search and the Keyword Planner to discover variations you may have missed.)

birth doula / labor support
childbirth classes / childbirth preparation classes / birthing classes
prenatal yoga classes / mother baby yoga classes / prenatal fitness

postpartum doula
breastfeeding support / breastfeeding consultant / breastfeeding counselor
placenta encapsulation

end-of-life doula / death doula / death midwife
home funeral guide
advance care planning facilitator

Keyword Placement

For each page on your website, or for each new blog post, you can designate a "focus keyword" or keyword phrase that you want that page to rank for. Do not use the same focus keywords on multiple pages. Each page should have its own unique focus. Your keywords should be included in the following places (brackets < > indicate html code):

- Page title, top header, <h1>
- Meta description (this can and should be customized)
- Major subheadings on the page <h2> and <h3>
- First paragraph of copy (make sure the topic is clear immediately)
- A couple of other times in the body of the page
- URL (or permalink) for the page
- Edit all images to include the "alt tag" and insert your chosen keywords here too.
- Include your best keywords in links, aka "anchor text" (e.g., make it "find a birth doula" rather than "click here to find a birth doula."

If you have a website and were not keyword aware when you created it, you can fix this. Just go in and work with each page, editing it to meet the SEO requirements. As a writer, I find it a bit frustrating to write for the keywords. It's not natural to think and express oneself in terms of keywords and, in many cases, I think it dumbs down what I have written. So be it. Better that my customers find me, and read what I have to offer, than develop a page which pleases me but attracts few readers because Google doesn't "see" me.

I use a plugin called "Yoast SEO" with a WordPress platform (recommended!) for my website. This plugin is very user friendly and designed to help you fully optimize your site for the search engines. Make sure this plugin (or something equivalent) gets activated on your website. It will guide you through the process of identifying your focus keyword and meta keywords, as well as editing the meta description. Next it performs a content analysis and basically gives you a grade on each parameter (green=good to go; orange=needs work; red=top and fix). The page then gets ranked accordingly. I like that this tool prompts me through the recommended fixes. I just keep at it until I get the green light. If you are using something other than WordPress for your site, then do a little searching online for SEO tools and tutorials designed to work with your chosen platform.

There are lots of strategies for optimizing your results with the search engines and this is an essentially fluid area of expertise rather than a static set of rules. Google is constantly changing the algorithms used to calculate page rank and several factors come into play. Ideally, engage a website designer who is SEO savvy and who can help you get it set up correctly from the start. Thereafter, SEO is an ongoing effort.

 See *The Doula Business Guide, 3rd Edition* for more strategies.

Sample

Let's sketch out a web page using **"placenta encapsulation"** as our **focus keyword.**

Page title <h1> = **Placenta Encapsulation** Services

Major subheadings <h2> =
- Benefits of **Placenta Encapsulation** (short introduction, bulleted list, links to research, more information)
- **Placenta Encapsulation** Services Offered (description of services, products available)
- How the **Placenta Encapsulation** Process Works (description)
- Cost of **Placenta Encapsulation** (prices)

Is there any room for doubt regarding what this web page is about? Include at least one picture on the page and imbed **placenta encapsulation** in the alt tag. A YouTube video of you demonstrating how to process a placenta would be a fabulous addition to this page. Never be afraid to share information. Most folks don't want to process their own placentas and are very happy to pay for this service. If you lose one or two because you showed them how to do it for themselves, no worries. The amount of traffic you can generate to your YouTube channel (and from there to your website) is worth it. You can also share the video on social media forums to generate buzz. Before you know it, you are a trusted authority.

Website Planning Checklist

TASKS	✔
Critique 5–10 doula websites: • What emotion does the site evoke? • Is the site easy or difficult to navigate (e.g., can you quickly find what you are looking for)? Why? Any frustrations? • Is the site pleasing, interesting or engaging? Why or why not? • What color palettes work best? • Is there any reason to ever return to this website (e.g., valuable content)? • What design elements do you like or not like? *Keep notes on your findings, along with the URLs, so that you can show examples of your preferences to your designer.*	
Create a "site map" • Navigation tool bar on homepage (what do you want here?) • What content will be on each page?	
Create content • Write up your content for each page. • This is best done in a Word file and then can easily be copied and pasted into the site once your designer has the framework set up. • Make it easy for people to find what they are looking for on the page; what's most important? • Identify the focus keyword/keyword phrase for each page. • Gather pictures, artwork or videos to enhance your site. • Get a great professional headshot of yourself and use it on the site. • Your full name and location should be on the homepage!	
Integrate SEO strategies	
Recommended extras • Mechanism for capturing email addresses of visitors to the site (aka "opt-in"), preferably located in the upper right-hand corner of the homepage • A "Links" page (could also be called favorite resources, community resources, recommendations, etc.) • Social media links to your Facebook business page/group, Instagram, Pinterest board, etc. • Add a shopping cart function and secure gateway for processing payments (may not need this at first).	

Whether all the components on your site work effectively together, or not, is really in the details. This checklist is designed to help you progress through the steps involved. It is not necessarily a linear process, so you do not need to do everything in the order listed. Your designer will be a synergistic part of this process and can also show you samples and templates and make suggestions. However, having a sense of what you want, like or don't like, will save you time (and money!) in the long run.

📖 *The Doula Business Guide 3ʳᵈ Edition* provides further guidance on considerations in creating a website, the design process and how to hire a designer.

SWOT Analysis Tool
Adapted from MindTools.com

The SWOT Analysis was originated by Albert S Humphrey in the 1960s as a technique for understanding your Strengths and Weaknesses, and for identifying both the Opportunities open to you and the Threats you face. Used in a business context, it helps the business owner carve out a sustainable market niche. Used in a personal context, it helps the individual develop his/her career in a way that takes best advantage of unique talents, abilities and opportunities.

> ## Niche
>
> a specialized segment of the market for a product or service;
> a comfortable or suitable position in life or employment

What makes the SWOT framework particularly powerful is that, with a little thought, it can help you uncover opportunities that you are well-placed to exploit. And, by understanding your weaknesses, you can manage and eliminate threats that might otherwise catch you unawares. Ideally, the tool will enable you to craft a strategy that helps you distinguish yourself from your competitors so that you can compete successfully in your market.

Explore your Strengths (internal positive factors; within your control)

- What do you do well?

- What do you do better than anyone else?

- What do others see as your strengths?

- What internal resources do you have (e.g., positive attributes of people, such as knowledge, background, education, credentials, network, reputation or skills)?

- What tangible assets do you have (e.g., capital, credit, existing customers or distribution channels)?

- What advantages do you have over your competition?

Consider your Weaknesses (internal negative factors; within your control)

- What could you improve?

- What factors detract from your ability to obtain or maintain a competitive edge?

- What does your business lack (e.g., expertise or access to skills)?

- What should you avoid?

- What are people in your market likely to see as weaknesses?

- What areas need improvement to compete with your strongest competitor?

- What factors lose you sales?

Explore any Opportunities (external positive factors; out of your control)

- What opportunities exist in your market or the environment that you can benefit from?

- What good opportunities can you spot?

- What trends can you take advantage of?

- How can you turn your strengths into opportunities?

- Can you create an opportunity by eliminating any of your weaknesses?

- Is the opportunity ongoing, or is there just a window for it? In other words, how critical is your timing?

Consider Potential Threats (external negative factors; out of your control)

- What obstacles do you face?

- Who are your existing or potential competitors? What are they doing well?

- Is changing technology threatening your position?

- What threats do your weaknesses expose you to?

- Are there challenges created by an unfavorable trend or development that may lead to deteriorating revenues?

- What factors beyond your control could place your business at risk?

Developing strategies from your SWOT

Once you have identified and prioritized your SWOT results, you can use them to develop short-term and long-term strategies for your business. The true value of this exercise is in using the results to maximize the positive influences on your business and minimize the negative ones. Consider how your strengths, weaknesses, opportunities and threats overlap with each other. For example, look at the strengths you identified and then come up with ways to use those strengths to maximize the opportunities. Then, look at how those same strengths can be used to minimize the threats you identified. Continuing this process, use the opportunities you identified to **develop strategies that will minimize the weaknesses** or **avoid the threats**. The following table can be used to help you organize the strategies in each area.

	Opportunities (external, positive)	**Threats** (external, negative)
Strengths (internal, positive)	**Strength-Opportunities Strategies** Which of your strengths can be used to maximize the identified opportunities?	**Strength-Threats Strategies** How can you use your strengths to minimize the threats?
Weaknesses (internal, negative)	**Weakness-Opportunity Strategies** What action(s) can you take to minimize your weaknesses using the identified opportunities?	**Weakness-Threats Strategies** How can you minimize your weaknesses to avoid external threats?

For some perspective …

It will likely be very helpful to invite a handful of associates who are close to you and your business to participate in your SWOT analysis. You will need to do the legwork up front (answer the questions), but then bring a few folks together for the analysis and planning.

Turning Challenges (Weaknesses and Threats) into Goal Statements

Examples

Challenge: Inconsistent registration numbers for childbirth classes
Goal: Enroll a minimum of six couples in all classes this year.

Challenge: Marketing/effective use of social media
Goal: Identify and implement three strategies to enhance my professional presence online this year.

Challenge: I'm feeling so overwhelmed with my to-do list, I don't even have time to integrate help.
Goal: By the end of the month I will identify three specific changes I can make to become more efficient and in control of my time.

Mastering the Sabotage Monster Within

Are you saying negative things to yourself about yourself? You will need to become the master of the *Sabotage Monster Within*—that voice of self-doubt in your head that tells you you're not good enough, experienced enough, smart or savvy. The good news is the Monster can only claim as much power as you allow. Would you let your clients beat themselves up with negative self-messages? Why do you deserve less?

I don't mean to imply here that we should not endeavor to address any shortcomings we may have. We can't *think* our way to becoming a more experienced doula; we need to provide services to more families, engaging the work in real time. We do, however, have complete control over how we think about our lack of experience, how we present ourselves, and what we choose to do about it.

If you are having a hard time signing clients once the initial interview is over, *be curious* about what is going on. Curiosity takes judgment and blame out of the equation. One simply reflects on the various encounters and adopts a non-defensive and open attitude—what is there for me to learn here? I can pose all kinds of possible factors in play, but here are a few basic principles that may be a common denominator for folks experiencing repeated disappointments.

- Are you arriving to interviews on time and prepared to make a positive, professional impression?
- Are you focused on the needs of the individual/family, demonstrating the heart of doula work, or are you more focused on yourself and the impression you are making (feeling nervous)?
- Is there any ambivalence in your mind about engaging doula work?
- Do you hear yourself giving any mixed messages?
- Do you second-guess yourself?
- Do you find yourself blaming others for your disappointments?
- Who is doing most of the talking at your interviews? (Hint: It should be the client.)

Re-programming ourselves or what we can do about it

- Avoid the toxic people in your life (or at least limit the amount of time you spend in their company). You know who they are. Anyone who reinforces self-doubt, who tries to drag you down, who might feel threatened if you succeed at your goals, who seems to be invested in you feeling poorly about yourself. Surround yourself instead with people who think you are awesome!

- Become an observer of your own thoughts. Keep your radar up for negative self-messages. Disengage from the emotion of the messages, step back and simply notice when you say something unloving to yourself. Becoming aware of our thoughts is the first step in reprogramming.

- Look for patterns of thinking, beliefs and behaviors that are not serving you well. Where do these patterns come from? How can you change these?

- Work with affirmations to address patterns you are trying to change (see pp. 15–16). Steep yourself in positive assertions regarding the changes you want to manifest. Affirmations work best when we state the intended result as fact.

> Say: "I have the perfect number of clients for me."
> Rather than: "I'm intending to get the perfect number of clients."
>
> Or "I weigh 150 pounds."
> Rather than "I plan to lose 35 pounds."

Repeat this message to yourself frequently. Write it down and post it around your house where you will see it. Say it out loud.

- Many folks benefit from professional counseling. Find a counselor who uses Cognitive Behavioral Therapy (CBT) and commit to the program. You will learn many useful techniques for managing anxiety, anger, victimization and more. CBT does not involve years of endless counseling sessions seeking to unpack and examine every childhood trauma. Rather, it provides tools for use in the present moment to better manage your emotions, responses and interactions with others in a way that works for you.

Worry is a prayer for what you don't want.

Other fixes to increase doula confidence

- Complete a professional doula certification process.
- Find a mentor (be prepared to pay for this, or at the very least, to do some work for your mentor; there needs to be a good exchange of energy both ways here).
- Volunteer or offer your doula services at a reduced fee in order to boost your numbers and your confidence.
- Take enhanced training workshops to fill in gaps in knowledge.
- Keep learning, always.
- Accept that it is humbling to learn a new skill in life, whether it's becoming a doula, learning to speak a foreign language or mastering a new dance step. It's hard to be in a position where we feel incompetent. Really hard, like puberty hard. But it is the only way we grow.

Cultivate courage!
(It's not courage if you're not afraid.)

Grounding Techniques

These simple techniques can be used anytime you are feeling anxious or overwhelmed. They might be employed before a public speaking event, going into a client interview or when meeting with your client to provide services for the first time. Suffering from a bad case of the butterflies (aka "performance anxiety")? *First, remember it's not about you. Focus on your clients and commit to doing your best for them.*

- Take five conscious, deep breaths. Inhale deeply and slowly, into your belly and exhale slowly, completely letting go of tension in your face, neck and shoulders. Take another deep, slow inhalation. Keep letting go, sinking your energy to just below your navel (what the Tai Chi masters refer to as the "dantian" or energy center of the body). Reign in your mind and stay focused on what you are doing. Each breath gets easier. With each breath you feel more grounded.

- When feeling vulnerable, check your body language and protect yourself. Are you sitting stoop-shouldered (weight of the world), radiating a "poor me" vibe, as though you expect to be under-appreciated, mistreated, taken advantage of? Sit up straight, shoulders back, sternum lifted and (most importantly) feet planted firmly on the ground. Fold your hands in your lap. This simple pose offers some protection. You don't expect to be heaped upon and you do not make an easy target (now it just rolls off your back). The clasped hands close your circle, making you less open and vulnerable.

- Imagine precisely what you want the outcome to be. You are not subject to what everyone else wants. Be clear. State your intentions out loud to yourself.

- When performance anxiety sets in or starts to take over your body (shaking, loose stools, upset stomach and so on), try some Rescue Remedy. For the uninitiated, Rescue Remedy is a combination of five Bach Flower Essences. It is taken from a dropper bottle and placed directly on the tongue or can be added to a beverage that you sip on. It is known for its calming, grounding effect and ability to head off panic attacks. Flower essences are vibrational in nature and perfectly safe for everyone—pregnant and breastfeeding mamas, doulas, children, pets, the dying … everyone!

- Practice gratitude. List/recite ten things that you are grateful for.

- If you believe in the power of prayer, ask for grace; you are not alone.

Fear and gratitude cannot occupy the same space.

Competition Makes Us Stronger

Really? Yes, it can, but that is up to you. Recently, I was feeling really irritated by new (and old) competitors in the doula training field and (embarrassingly) heard myself moaning and complaining, bitching and whining. It wasn't pretty, I must say. This is the dark side and it will bring out the worst in us, but only if we get stuck there or are looking for an excuse to fail. I'd like to think that I command the high road, that worrying about competition is beneath me. That competition is, in fact, moot. The truth is, the irritation I experience is necessary for growth. It stimulates vital change. So, go ahead and grouse (if you need to) and get it out of your system, preferably in a non-public way. Then shake it off and take a fresh look.

In response to two different perceived threats recently, and after much consideration, I raised my rates across the board. Considerably. I acknowledge it's a leap of faith, but it feels right. Within hours of putting the new rates up on my website, I made two sales and took this as validation. Instead of giving way to fear, jealousy (ouch), anger—be curious! Our competitors force us to consider: What are they doing that is resonating with our shared target audience that I am not? What is special or different about my business? Do I have a niche that gives me a special boost?

5 Steps to Defining your Niche Market

> ### What is a "Niche Market"?
>
> A niche is a subset of a market that you have identified as having some special characteristic. A niche does not exist per se, but rather is created by identifying needs and wants that are being addressed poorly or not at all by your competitors and then developing and delivering goods or services to satisfy them.

Step 1. Identify your ideal customer and be as specific as you can (see Exercise on pp. 83–86).

Step 2. Consider your achievements and what it is that you do best. Return to our Personal Inventory Exercise (pp. 5–10) and review your skills and strengths.

Step 3. Talk with prospective customers and identify their main concerns. Try to see the world through their eyes.

Step 4. Synthesize your answers to the first three steps. Your niche should arise naturally from your interests and experience, and your clients' needs and wants. What do you naturally gravitate towards? How can you create something new?

Step 5. Evaluate your idea. A good niche meets the following criteria:

- It takes you where you want to go—in other words, it conforms to your long-term vision.
- Your customers want it.
- It's carefully planned.
- It's one-of-a-kind, unique among your competitors.
- It evolves, allowing you to develop different profit centers and still retain the core business, thus ensuring long-term success.

Being Different

Here's another way to think about the problem …

> ### 3 Questions
>
> Can you sell *something* different?
> Can you meet the unmet needs of *someone* different?
> Can you sell something *differently?*

Here are a couple of examples …

Example 1

A business downtown sells Christmas trees every year. Competition from the mega stores and strip malls is fierce as these competitors have tons of free parking available and can charge lower prices due to lower rent costs where they are located. Our savvy downtown business owner sets up a tree wrapper in the middle of the yard and engages his customers' children to "help" him catch the tree when it comes out of the wrapper. Nothing is actually required of the children, but they think it is great to watch the tree come out of the wrapper and pretend to help guide it in the right direction. Then they are all invited to help themselves to an orange and a candy cane.

My son was relating the "story" of buying the Christmas tree with his three little ones in tow. Do you think he will go back to the downtown store next year (paying more in the process for his tree)? You bet he will. He got more than a mere Christmas tree for his money; he got a fun experience with his kids. Next consider, how many people do you think he told his story to? I'm guessing more than just me. This business owner figured out how to sell his product *differently.* And the niche he has claimed overcomes price resistance.

Example 2

I have run a childbirth education center since 1998. In recent years, we experienced a downward trend in enrollments which was noted by other providers locally and reflected on the national scene as well. Sadly, my own sons and their wives did not take me up on my offer of free classes when they were expecting due to conflicting work schedules! This new generation of childbearing parents is fundamentally different than the previous generation and it seems they are juggling more than ever before.

I began to ponder the three questions: How could I sell something different, or sell to someone different, or sell differently? One day an idea literally popped into my head, pretty much fully formed: childbirth classes online for busy couples, moms on bedrest and folks who are not in my backyard. (Online options are abundant now, but several years ago, there were very few online classes on the market and these were mostly comprised of web pages filled with text and perhaps a few pictures. I knew I could do it better.)

My idea was different because it represented a new product, one I hadn't offered before. The "who" was different because distance is not a factor; anyone can benefit from my wisdom! And it is sold differently, that is online. Thus, I ended up hitting all three ways of adapting my business to meet changing market trends, when only one is required. Plus, the new venture met all the criteria for a good niche listed above. Primarily, it took me where I wanted to go, playing to my passion and strengths (I love to write and create curricula). Another overarching business goal for me continues to be increasing passive income streams, that is, income from products that are a fait accompli; nothing further required on my end. So, this was a good idea from pretty much any angle. It has worked out well, despite the explosion in competition on this front. Unanticipated (bonus) benefits include:

1. Folks who take our in-person classes can make up any missed classes with comparable material online (no one else in my area offers this).
2. We now have the option to offer a combination of online and hands-on learning, leaving class time for more interactive and fun learning activities, a win-win-win scenario.
3. I now have tons of online content that can be used for marketing purposes as well. I can extract special reports, questionnaires, demonstrations videos and more for a variety of promotional needs.

P.S. The amount of work involved in taking this idea from vision to reality was truly daunting. But I kept plugging away at it and, eventually, I had a product.

Grow a bigger pie!

Back to our beliefs about money, abundance and scarcity. The business owner with a scarcity mindset freaks out every time there is a change in the marketplace. She is upset that so-and-so just came to town and set up a competing doula business. Or she is seriously thrown for a loop after hearing that two experienced doulas have teamed up and formed a new doula agency. When others make changes, it rocks her boat and robs her of peace of mind. Her lack of equanimity is based in a belief that there is a finite number of people in her community who are willing to invest in hiring a doula. If the overall size of the pie is limited and a competitor helps herself to a slice of it, then your slice just got smaller. Right? Wrong!

That's not how it works. More doulas practicing and getting the word out create a bigger pie. An abundance mindset embraces a welcoming attitude toward other doulas. More families will hear about the benefits of doulas. There is plenty for all and great potential for all of us to continue to grow our businesses. Mine doesn't get smaller because you are successful. But I might need to change it up a bit, find my niche and get creative.

Are You Feeling Stuck?

Failing to achieve your goals and objectives?
Having a hard time getting anything done?

Instead of beating yourself up, let's be curious about the reasons.

What's going on?

What else is on your plate in addition to your business?

Are your goals and timelines reasonable or overly ambitious?

Are you struggling with procrastination? Do any of the following reasons resonate with you?

1. Laziness (You might not be cut out to be self-employed.)
2. Fear of failure (What's the worst that can happen?)
3. Perfectionism. (Consider the possibility that _____ "is good enough.")

If there is one thing that is within your power to make life easier right now, what would that be?

Are there any other practical supports you can think of that would help you be more productive (e.g., help with childcare, a functional work space)?

Would you benefit from more training such as a workshop, book, webinar or coaching session? Identify areas where you would reap an immediate benefit from more knowledge or guidance.

Are there new habits you could foster that would help with productivity (e.g., go to bed earlier/later, get a "work buddy")?

Deadlines help most of us get things done. When you are your own boss, deadlines may come and go without clear-cut consequences if they are not met. Who are you accountable to? How can you build accountability into your business?

No one else can get you unstuck.
You are going to have to figure it out for yourself
and take necessary action.

How to Form a Mastermind Group

What is a Mastermind Group?

The concept of the Mastermind was introduced by Napoleon Hill in the early 1900s. In his timeless classic *Think and Grow Rich*, he wrote about the Mastermind principle as:

The coordination of knowledge and effort of two or more people, who work toward a definite purpose, in the spirit of harmony.

No two minds ever come together without thereby creating a third, invisible intangible force, which may be likened to a third mind [the mastermind].

Today, many entrepreneurs have discovered that being a small business owner can be a somewhat lonely undertaking. Not so much when we are engaged in the work of our business providing services to customers, but undeniably when it comes time to work *on* our businesses. The Mastermind concept provides a solution. It offers a combination of brainstorming, education, peer accountability and support to help group members achieve success. It provides the following benefits:

- Encouragement to set and achieve business goals
- Constructive feedback
- Creative synergy of the group
- Supportive community of fellow business owners who understand the challenges
- Catalyst for growth

How does it work?

A group of entrepreneurs join forces to work on their businesses. The available meeting time is equally divided among the members and a timer is set when each member's time begins. The Mastermind works best when members come prepared with something specific for the group to consider. For example, it could be a request for feedback on a new webpage or rack card, brainstorming promotional ideas, or exploring the pros and cons of adding new products or services. Each participant benefits from the undivided attention of all group members when it's her/his turn and, in turn, gives her/his full focus to others when it's their turn. Often, there are tips, ideas and strategies that are beneficial for all, no matter how different the businesses may be. The group supports accountability because, at the end of your time, your next steps and goals can be set. People who come, month after month, unprepared and falling short of goals will ultimately be weeded out of the group because it will be embarrassing to continue making excuses and they will be a drag on the group's energy.

There are several variations on how the Mastermind can work. One is to have a cross-industry group. It pretty much doesn't matter what the business is, because marketing and growth strategies that work for one kind of business can often be adapted for many other kinds of businesses. The first group I participated in was male dominated and included a heating and cooling business owner, a restaurant owner, a carpet cleaner, a physical therapist, a marketing specialist, a landscape architect and a lawyer. One of the big benefits of working with this group was the varied male perspectives that forced me to question my assumptions. Plus, they could give me a guy's perspective on marketing childbirth classes to expectant couples (not something I had sought prior to joining the group). This group really shook me up and forced me out of my self-limiting thought bubble.

Another variation is to gather a group of industry-specific entrepreneurs (e.g., maternal-infant health professionals or aging/end-of-life specialists), though it is essential to avoid direct competitors in the same group. For example, in the maternal-infant health focused group, you could have a homebirth midwife, a lactation consultant in private practice, a childbirth educator, a birth doula, a postpartum doula, a photographer, a wellness coach and so on. The advantage here lies in a shared awareness of useful resources and venues for exposure potentially relevant to all group members. In this instance, you are all industry insiders.

Groups may be free and leaderless, or you might find a group in your area that is led by a facilitator who charges a fee to guide the group.

A Mastermind group is not ...

- *A class.* While your group can vote to bring in guest speakers occasionally, the primary focus is the brainstorming and accountability support among the group members.
- *Group coaching.* Mastermind groups are about the members sharing with each other. It is not about one facilitator coaching individuals in a group setting. You get everyone's feedback, advice and support and the conversation is balanced among all the group members.
- *A networking group.* While you may share leads and resources with each other, it is not the intent of the meetings.

What do you need?

- Ideally, four to six serious business owners; businesses can be loosely related but avoid directly competing businesses
- Mutual trust and a promise of confidentiality
- A commitment to participate fully (attend regularly, come prepared with your own problem or marketing piece, and be willing to give your full attention and best effort to others when it's their turn)
- A private space to meet with internet access and a lack of interruptions
- A regular monthly meeting time that works for all the members

Tips

- Keep in mind that the more members you have, the longer the time spent in the meeting or the shorter time available per individual. In my experience, a half an hour per person is just about perfect. It often takes at least five minutes to explain what it is you are doing and what you want help with. Then you are left with enough time to gather the desired feedback and brainstorm ideas.

- Too few members (two or three) is better than nothing, but a critical mass of at least four enhances the creative synergy of the group. Based on years of experience with two different groups, I think five members and a three-hour meeting is just about perfect. We set aside a bit of time at the beginning of the meeting to settle in, grab some tea and briefly check in with each other. There can also be a bathroom break about halfway through.

- Look for folks who are serious about their business and committed to the group. Over time, the group can become a powerful force for success in your life.

- Set a timer when each member starts their time. It should be set to go off five minutes before their time expires so they have a warning to wrap it up.

- Each member brings copies of any print materials they want critiqued. It's helpful if folks bring their laptops for critiquing web pages or other online materials.

- Don't worry if group members are all relatively new to marketing, the blind leading the blind. You can learn together, and you probably know more than you think. After all, you are a consumer and you know what works and doesn't work on you. Oftentimes, we just need someone to ask us the right question or point out that the way we have organized information on a web page is confusing, or say, "I don't know what this means." That second and third set of eyes can see what we cannot.

- If the group incorporates diversity in experience and skill level, that can be a good thing. However, if one group member is routinely having to mentor others who don't make an effort to provide return value, then that person is likely to become disenchanted with the energy exchange.

- Once you have a group that gels well together and meets reliably (this can take a while), you can close the group and just let it mature for a time. Be careful and thoughtful about admitting new members. In my group, we have agreed to run a name by the group before extending any invitations. If there are no objections and everyone is in agreement, then we may invite that individual. At this point, about ten years in, we are a functional tight group, so we would have to seriously consider whether adding a person will truly enhance the value of the group.

Infractions to Avoid
- Coming late to meetings.
- Accepting phone calls or text messaging during meetings.
- Going first in the round and then leaving the meeting before everyone has had their turn.

Marketing Plan Checklist

TASKS*	✔
Describe your ideal customer.	
Identify your Unique Selling Proposition (What makes you stand out from the crowd?)	
Create a website.	
Identify three strategies for making professional connections (aka networking) and cultivating referrals.	
Identify three outreach events or venues for reaching your target customers.	
Create a business card and (perhaps) rack cards.	
Pursue every possibility for getting free listings online.	
Create a media contacts list.	
Stage a social media strategy (create a Facebook business page or Pinterest board; open an Instagram account; join relevant groups; engage on the forums, and so on). *To be fair, this last item is not really a checklist item because it is complex, always changing, ongoing, and there are several venue choices. While some readers may be savvy, others may be (more or less) terrified. Your "strategy" should start with where you are today and your next three steps to move the bar a little higher.*	

Seven Characteristics of a True Professional

1. *Put your customers first.* Understanding and satisfying your customers' needs are the top priority. Value each customer and do your best for them.

2. *Become an expert in your chosen field.* The very word *professional* implies that you are an expert. Master the skills necessary to do your job and keep your knowledge up to date.

3. *Have integrity.* Behave in an ethical, respectful, trustworthy manner to others (including competitors, medical personnel and other professionals) and deliver on your promises.

4. *Communicate effectively.* Resist the urge to blame the customer when communication goes awry. Effective communication is ultimately your responsibility, not your customers'. Whether verbal or written, professionals communicate clearly, concisely, thoroughly and accurately.

5. *Praise your peers not yourself.* There is nothing more unprofessional and self-serving than telling others how wonderful you are. Professionals are humble and generous in their praise of others.

6. *Share your knowledge.* Information isn't a limited resource. It *is* possible to share what you know *and* stay one step ahead of the competition. Professionals help their peers and are respected for doing so.

7. *Be resourceful.* You don't have to know all the answers; you just need to know how to find the information or help you need. Professionals are lifelong learners.

Part 5
Additional Resources

Online Resources

Free Stuff

My first entry here is not really a resource, just some advice. There is a lot of great, free guidance available to you. Do some web browsing, using different keywords. You will find any number of marketing or business gurus. Pick one or two with whom you resonate and sign up for their newsletters, follow their blogs or join their Facebook groups. That way, regular, informative and inspiring content will show up in your Inbox so you can always be learning, but with very little effort and in small chunks.

Google Alerts

Use Google Alerts to help identify interesting new content on the web. This tool can be set up to email you notifications any time Google finds new results on a topic of interest. Here's how:

1. Visit www.google.com/alerts
2. In the "create an alert about" box, enter the keywords for which you want to receive notifications.
3. Click "show options" to say how often you get alerts, what types of results you want to get, and more.
4. Click "create alert."

For example, you could create an alert for "doula business" and your specialty (e.g., "end-of-life doulas").

Best of the Web

17Hats.com
Online tool for business organization.

AuthenticPromotion.com
Publishes a free e-newsletter on marketing, as well as other resources, for entrepreneurs. Sign up for the newsletter and get a 31-page guide, "The 12 Principles of Authentic Promotion."

Bloom Business Solutions
BloomBirthPros.com
Complete doula business system offers customizable form templates, worksheets, courses, website design and more.

BulletJournal.com
The Bullet Journal is a customizable organizational tool. It can be your to-do list, sketchbook and notebook.

CaféPress.com
Will imprint products with business name, logos, slogans (e.g., t-shirts, coffee mugs, bumper stickers, etc.).

LeonieDawson.com
Your Shining Biz & Life workbooks.

Define Your Marvelous Brand with Suzi Istvan
SocialSuziDesigns.com
Great marketing information; sign up for e-newsletter and free booklet.

DoulaMatch.net
Widely used referral website for birth and postpartum doulas. Basic listings are free; upgrade to an enhanced listing for a fee.

Dummies.com
Marketing your small business for dummies cheat sheet.

Evernote.com
Cloud application can be easily used on all devices. Uses the concept of digital "notebooks," like folders on your computer.

Facebook.com
There are a few groups on Facebook that are focused on the business side of being a doula (do a search). Go ahead and join a couple of them and explore a little till you find one or two that you like. You may also find reviews or recommendations for different apps and resources. Look for (and join!) relevant doula member groups in your local community. These are great for making connections and identifying local resources.

Internal Revenue Service
IRS.gov
Apply for an Employer Identification Number (EIN) online. Tax forms and instructions available as PDF files.

Nolo.com
Legal solutions website; provides a great deal of accessible information regarding business models and the nitty-gritty "how to" details of various models. Good, detailed information on business-related legal questions of all kinds.

PassionPlanner.com
Organize your business goals; free downloads available.

Small Business Administration
SBA.gov
U.S. government agency that provides support for entrepreneurs and small business owners. Great information for sorting out business structures and much more.

VistaPrint.com
Create business cards, rack cards, signs, banners, posters, etc.

WaveApps.com
Free invoicing and accounting software.

Wordtracker.com
Quickly identify your best-performing keywords.

Your State Government's Website
www.[StateName].gov
Provides information on developing a business plan, ways to legally structure a business and register a business name, licenses and permits required, and more.

YourDoulaBiz
Doula business management online platform.

Phone Apps
- MileIQ (mileage tracker)
- Prenatal Patient Tracker
- Spending (app for iPhone; for tracking business expenses)

Recommended Reading

Brennan, P. (2019). *The Doula Business Guide, 3rd Edition.* Ann Arbor, MI: Dream Street Press.

Covey, S. (2004) *7 Habits of Successful People: Powerful Lessons in Personal Change.* New York, NY: Free Press.

Gerber, M. (2001) *The E-Myth Revisited: Why Most Small Businesses Don't Work and What to Do about It.* New York: HarperCollins.

Gladwell, M. (2000) *The Tipping Point: How Little Things Can Make a Big Difference.* New York: Back Bay Books.

Godin, S. (2002) *Purple Cow: Transform Your Business by Being Remarkable.* New York, NY: Penguin Group.

Hamilton, R.J. (2014) *The Millionaire Master Plan: Your Personalized Path to Financial Success.* New York, NY: Hachette Book Group.

Hayden, C. and Levinson, J. (2013) *Get Clients Now! A 28-Day Marketing Program for Professionals, Consultants and Coaches, 3rd Edition.* New York, NY: AMACOM.

Hill, N. (1937) *Think and Grow Rich.* Book is now in the public domain with many different publishers.

Kingston, K. (1999) *Clear Your Clutter with Feng Shui: Free Yourself from Physical, Mental, Emotional and Spiritual Clutter Forever.* New York, NY: Broadway Books.